# THE BOOK OF THE SCRIBE

# THE BOOK OF THE SCRIBE

**LANCE KENNEDY**

ARKTOS
LONDON 2025

**ARKTOS**
🌐 Arktos.com   fb.com/Arktos   arktosmedia   arktosjournal

Copyright © 2025 by Arktos Media Ltd.

All rights reserved. No part of this book may be reproduced or utilised in any form or by any means (whether electronic or mechanical), including photocopying, recording or by any information storage and retrieval system, without permission in writing from the publisher.

**ISBN**
978-1-917646-63-5 (Paperback)
978-1-917646-64-2 (Hardback)
978-1-917646-65-9 (Ebook)

**Editing**
Constantin von Hoffmeister

**Layout**
Tor Westman

FOREWORD

# A GOSPEL OF FIRE AND EMPIRE

by Constantin von Hoffmeister

BLOOD, SCRIPTURE, the grand narrative of power torn from chaos — *The Book of the Scribe* is a manuscript of myth, war, and the broken covenant of man. It is a weapon, a codex of defiance, a scripture etched in battle-worn hands. The world it unfolds is not some genteel esoteric treatise. It is a clash of forces, an empire lost, a kingdom remembered. It is the stuff of prophets and destroyers, of tongues that burn while uttering the essential, of the ever-turning cycle of rise and ruin, bound together in apocalyptic revelation. To read it is to take up arms against the encroaching darkness. To wield it is to believe. And belief, as we have always known, is the first and last battle.

There is something in its pages that echoes Robert E. Howard's Hyborian Age — a lost kingdom of men crushed by the merciless tsunami of time and treachery. The rise of empires, their inevitable dissolution into myth, and the lone figure — half warrior, half prophet — who stands against the abyss. But where Howard's Conan is a man of flesh and sinew, *The Book of the Scribe* moves beyond the merely human; it speaks in the language of gods, of Guardians, of the ultimate contest between the forces of All and the devourer None. It is the primal American story told not with the detached hand of the historian but with the fevered intensity of one who has seen the fall, who has beheld Zion laid low and seeks, through blood and scripture, to raise it again.

This where the frontier bleeds into divinity. America, the land of lost tribes and endless horizons, of prophets driven from empire, of sacred texts scrawled on golden plates, hidden in mountains, revealed in fragments to the desperate and the chosen alike. The Book of Mormon, with its tales of exile and return, of the righteous driven westward, of kingdoms split and devoured by their own hubris, resonates here as well. It is the same vision: the holy city, the empire that could have been, the cycle that must be broken. *The Book of the Scribe* is the continuation of an old, old battle. It is a promise made in dust and betrayal, in a land where walls rose to block out the light and the unworthy sought power beyond their station.

This is scripture as war, as conquest, as the birthright of those who refuse to kneel. Its words do not instruct; they command. The foundation of its world is the foundation of every world where men have fought to defy the void. The Guardians — ancient, ascended, yet bound to the fate of man — stand at the heart of it, their will shaping the march of history. They do not grant wisdom freely; it must be seized, claimed, lived. It is the old law, the law of the strong, the law of those who choose to stand beneath the Seven Mountains and remember what was stolen. This is the rage of the fallen empire, the fury of the exiled, the fire that does not go out.

To those who would see in it only a fantasy, a fable of battle and exile, I say: look again. This is no child's tale, no escapist's dream. This is the heartbeat of the West, the howl of the last free men before they are buried beneath the weight of None. This is a warning. This is an elegy. This is a call to arms. The book does not ask for interpretation; it asks for allegiance. You cannot stand at the walls and pretend neutrality. You must decide whether to build them higher or tear them down.

Howard's warriors — Conan, Kull, Bran Mak Morn — each carried the burden of a dying world, the knowledge that civilization was an edifice destined to crumble. *The Book of the Scribe* carries this same burden, but it does not accept the end so easily. This is not the song of a man who watches Rome burn and turns away. This is the testament of one who reaches into the fire, who would rather be consumed than allow the city to fall unavenged. It is a war against apostasy, the eternal struggle against the Great and Abominable Church. It is the Manifest Destiny of the spirit, a kingdom not only remembered but restored.

And here, as with all true scripture, is the hero who does not only wield the sword but also wields the word. Mithra, the Scribe, whose name carries the weight of prophecy, whose book is both a record and a weapon, is no passive chronicler. He is both warrior and oracle, both prophet and avenger. In this, he reminds us of the figures of Joseph Smith and Nephi, of Conan and Bran Mak Morn, of every leader who has understood that history does not wait for the meek. He is the last defense against None, against the gnawing nothingness that seeks to consume the light. His words are not an attempt to understand history but to remake it.

For this is the purpose of all true scripture: to create the world anew. *The Book of the Scribe* does not rest in the past; it reaches forward, towards the empire that must rise again. It speaks to those who do not accept the fall as final, who believe that Zion may yet be restored. It is revelation, not as gentle speech but as furious battle cry. It is the blood of nations scrawled onto the pages of eternity, an oath that the West will not go quietly.

So, for those who open these pages, know this: You are not simply reading. You are bearing witness. The words you see here are not meant to sit idly in the mind; they are meant to stir the will, to move the hand, to awaken the warrior. This is not entertainment. This is war. This is the final march of the faithful, the battle that will determine whether the light still burns in the hearts of men.

You will read. You will decide. You will choose whether to wield the word, whether to join the Scribe, whether to stand beneath the Seven Mountains and remember. The empire was lost. The empire may rise again. This book is not just a record of that battle. It is the battle itself.

Now, the battle begins.

Frankfurt am Main, Germany,<br>12 February 2025

"The lion addresses me: 'We guard day and night and hold passage to deeper mysteries. Do you carry the Word for entering the sanctuary's upper halls?' I reply, 'I do not, but the Guardians have it.'"

—16.10.5–6

## 0

0. In the name of the Scribe, Bridger of the Way, Mouth of the Guardians:

1. These are the words of power from the ultimate and generative source.

2. He who first hears and accepts them and then lives by their tenets shall never succumb to None, but will wield strength and power as a two-edged sword.

3. Great is he who grasps this mighty wisdom, for he will be fortified and stand as an unbreakable fortress!

4. May the might of All be with the steadfast and honored warriors who trust in the Way of the Scribe and uphold it with unwavering resolve.

5. May the Will of All shield and empower you against every dark assault and the snares of None.

6. May the wisdom of the Guardians fortify your heart and reveal your legend.

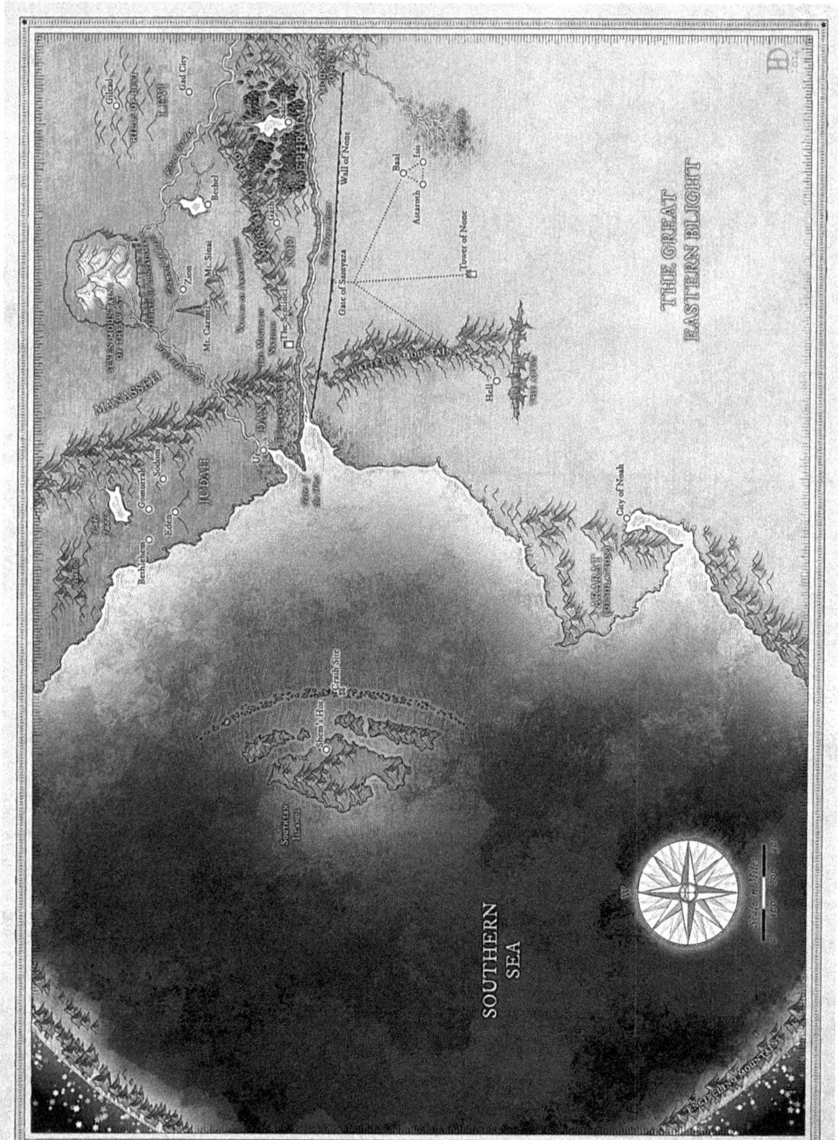

FULL COLOR VERSION

# THE FOUNDATION OF THE SCRIBE

## 1

1. These are our words, the words of the Guardians who defeated None and his kin
2. We are they who are in heaven and inside the Seven Mountains of the West
3. Guardians we are of creation, and yes, once we were but imperfect men
4. For all is One and we are of All, all is connected and moves ever high
5. We see all lowly creatures ascend upward in this universal pattern
6. As we once did when we were born from the womb, the living will rise to the sky
7. They will become All with all the supreme powers that we have always possessed
8. All power flows from All, for all is One, but must be tapped to be used by some
9. We may be higher than they who are below, but we are all connected: One
10. Power flows equally through All and may be taken by any that wants
11. Perception is the only thing that changes and not the power possessed in

12. Biology the hindering block for all begotten creatures and children
13. Once you die and arise from the tomb of life, you obtain All and hate None
14. We are not like the eons of the made worlds; we understood more and found All
15. As you are low, so are we to those who are All and who determine our fate
16. Rising from nothing into the light, we achieved greatness, but not the finish
17. Our passage as ones below ends with an end, yet will arise to a new height
18. As we have done, the creatures of the earth create in a limited fashion
19. Creating is in being and expands with each life, newfound parameters
20. We founded the world and designed its fate from the beginning to the next end

21. We exited the Halls of the Dead and came out of the void of chaos
22. Launching ourselves on a ride of calamity, we escaped the expanse
23. And began the work of creating something that All has forever done
24. Bringing forth matter from nothing and establishing the laws of nature
25. Many universes formed, and the high dimensions expanded outward
26. We were the seething storm high above the waters of the dead creation
27. The universe of men began ages and ages ago in the past
28. The greatness of years before the crimson dawning of man and his empire
29. Before his whole world fell around him, with his walls collapsing as he watched

30. Spoke life into being after the stars collided through the course of time
31. Through man's earliest living ancestors until he sprang to conscious life
32. Instinct to reason to consciousness in its limited ability
33. The first command was to do what he willed and to aid evolution
34. To establish an empire near the tomb of the bright sun and of the sky
35. Where the home of the Guardians would be the Seven Mountains of the West
36. For Zion was, but it was not to last for the curse of None the Dragon
37. On the edges of the universe, imperfection condensed into None
38. And once in the form of the Dragon he is he descended upon man

39. Then we felt the jolt in the expanses around by None's arrival
40. But still, our perfect plan went ahead, not assaulted or hindered
41. The base animal man progressed unhindered by any desire
42. He went forth out in the fields before the Seven Mountains of the West
43. Tilling the black soil, the growing of the empire commanded of him
44. Man grew and never feared, for he lived in the light of the Western sun
45. But Zion's peace was not to last as all existences have their end
46. None seeing the promise of the empire and us, the Guardians
47. Came to our creation and dreamed of its destruction and of man's end
48. He was envious of what we had made and protected in the West
49. And established his dark kingdom in the eastern corner of the world
50. As King None is nothing in bodily form, he was our enemy
51. So, our reaction was to curse the East, divide it by a river
52. A blight would spread across his infernal land and a desert it was

53. We raised the massive cliffs of the west on the west side of the river
54. The cliffs shaded the dark land of King None from the beauty of the west
55. We spared our bright creation and the view of his nothingness and hate

56. None was envious of Western glory and the blessings of men
57. And of the power that the beyond granted us, the Guardians
58. He made a mockery of our creation by bringing forth None's children
59. The Watchers in his blighted and horrible Kingdom of the East
60. From nothingness into existence to destroy the world of men
61. Mocking the made river, they bridged it and irrigated his land
62. He built a wall from north to south in opposition to Our cliffs
63. None's children did his bidding and founded his eastern tower there
64. So, they might see the light that shone from the Seven Mountains for man
65. But their plans failed, and jealousy filled the emptiness of their souls
66. Brooding, sullen on the top of his tower, the Dragon waited
67. For a chance to assail the protected high valleys of the west
68. Knowing that men would desire sight of what was hidden from their eyes
69. The secret darkness of the eastern blight and None's horrid tower
70. The Watchers of None waited for the chance that was to come to them
71. And with the coming of Cain, the doom of the empire was sealed

72. The cliffs we had made were like all things of the world, imperfect
73. Limited in their fashion and, if misused, were set to fail
74. Imperfection: if descended, their secrets would be opened
75. Cain and his wife desired to see the hidden darkness

76. And left the protected valleys under the Seven Mountains
77. To gain a glimpse of the desert, its walls, and darkened tower
78. They came to the cliffs and began their descent to the river
79. Giving up our secret paths within the cliffs to the Watchers
80. Then they crossed the river employing None's newly built bridges
81. And became the Nephilim of the east, the corrupted children
82. For None to use in his attack on the men of the valleys
83. There, Cain and his wife were taught by None to hate our Western light
84. And sent couriers back to the empire to corrupt their brethren
85. By telling them that they should place their trust in walls built up high
86. To block the light of the mountains so they could see the darkness

87. The beguiled men of the empire heeded Cain's instructions
88. And the children of the Seven Mountains built walls so tall
89. That it blocked the light of our mountains from our land
90. As man forsook the Guardians and chose his walls instead
91. To find protection against the Dragon and his children
92. He lost it all for the way shown by Cain was used by None
93. To attack man now unaided by the light of the West
94. Blinded by the words of the Nephilim, Cain, and his wife
95. The dimmed empire was no longer protected by on high
96. But was to fall from the evil within its golden gates
97. And the mighty Watchers threw themselves upon man's stone walls
98. And destroyed our kingdom of men to make them all their slaves
99. Scattering man far to the four points of the compass rose
100. Yet this only sealed their doom by releasing our light

101. The empire of the righteous had fallen to ruin
102. And its once lofty walls have now been felled by hatred
103. Its towers pulled down and trampled upon by evil
104. As None unsealed all vice, and his armies came to fight

105. The men of the downfall speak with no hope of triumph
106. The light of the empire, the Seven Western Mountains
107. Burn with their eternal glow and shall never perish
108. But for the chosen, this dominion was truly lost
109. When he scattered our children to the ends of the Earth
110. Once they lost their crowns of virginity on that night
111. The empire was gone, but another would spring again
112. For fire is the best fertilizer and death reward
113. New forests will grow where the old have long passed away

114. Listen now, you fallen and children of the scorn
115. We are beings who will ever be in heaven
116. Those who have decreed the judgment of your end's end
117. You are living in the days of tribulation
118. The days that sequel the fall of the great empire
119. The days of mighty reckoning and clashing swords
120. You think you gained victory over the high West
121. You earned defeat, for we are calling our tribes
122. We will raise the empire from its condemnation
123. Its walls restored, and its temple baptized by fire
124. The sun will ever rise in the east and ere west
125. Your evil will fail, and its tale will be of hate

126. Azazel, Samyaza and the Nephilim
127. The Dragon sent them to quickly corrupt men
128. By telling them that they are all divided
129. The Grand Duke of None and the Destroyer now
130. Come to divide men and hence divide the One
131. None threw open his gates, and evil came forth
132. Revealed in the form of the fallen angels
133. We did not stop their coming, for men must halt
134. The advancement of None who will enslave them
135. The threat of separation was just enough

136. To make man ambitious and to save himself

137. The serpent seeks those who do not heed this
138. The demon regent in this creation
139. He sent his Watchers to reclaim the world
140. Infecting it all with his prideful lust
141. We on the Seven Mountains of the West
142. Look downward upon those being tempted
143. Giving them a celestial message
144. Written on the luminaries on high
145. Trying to bring it all back together
146. For division is not the final end

147. We speak wisdom to those who will hear
148. And know what they think when they come close
149. Throwing away excellence and pride
150. Before the coming of the Hero
151. The low will be blessed, and not the high
152. For the low listen and not corrupt
153. The works of our hands called the chosen
154. Will be gathered again together
155. But will go back to conquer the world

156. They march forward with hearts of steel
157. Following the path laid before them
158. Bringing hope to all the nations
159. And ending the dark age of None
160. Strength and justice shall rule the world
161. The lost shall be found, freed, and armed
162. Life shall flourish under new light
163. The Scribe will guide the holy war

164. You, the Tribes of Israel
165. 12,000 each have come here

166. Jude, Reuben, Levi, Asher,
167. Gad, Issachar, Zebulon,
168. Naphtali and Benjamin,
169. Manasseh and Simeon,
170. Dual blessing of Joseph

171. We are one with the Earth
172. We are the seething storm
173. Come near and find the One
174. But some will never try
175. We hide inside the minds
176. The spirits of soldiers

177. Like souls of children
178. And back, men may go
179. From darkness to light
180. Feeble wanderings
181. Into precious light

182. Your souls reborn
183. And trails have come
184. To make you men
185. One time again

186. We speak truth
187. And not the
188. Lies of them

189. We are
190. All One

191. One

192. Is All
193. Not None

194. We brought light
195. To the dark
196. And shadow

197. By extending
198. Fathering hands
199. Into the darkness
200. We brought forth life

201. In everything
202. In all existence
203. On every planet
204. In every being
205. Every chosen

206. None hindered us as we
207. Sought to join our Makers
208. Upward, upward we go
209. Then, into perfect bliss
210. Through the Halls of the Dead
211. And through infinite realms

212. The ashes of the downfall
213. Mixed with the blood of children
214. And ran down the broken walls
215. As carrion ate the dead
216. No hope for men of the West
217. Could be found in their tried hearts
218. For they were slaves of King None

219. The coming of None and his kin
220. Brought an end to a golden age
221. Marked by our temple in Zion
222. And the scattering of its tribes

223. To the four corners of the world
224. With some being taken as slaves
225. For the building of a city
226. Whose then dread name was Babylon

227. The Nephilim of Cain and his wife
228. Were made the regents of their brothers
229. Watching their work as they built new walls
230. And knowing we were in our mountains
231. They were watching as our empire fell
232. Seeing the plight of our beloved
233. And knowing that their end was to come
234. They prepared for war that was to come
235. With the free men who were yet to come

236. None was king of all the world; it did seem
237. From his tower in the eastern desert
238. To the foothills of the Seven Mountains
239. On top of the city Zion that once stood
240. He planned for his capital, Babylon
241. His citadel of power in the West
242. Out of which, he ordered forth his legions
243. To destroy resistance that might exist
244. For he was always afraid of the light
245. Truth from the Seven Mountains of the West

246. The light that came from the Seven High Mountains
247. That once was blocked out by Cain's infernal walls
248. Was spread across the old Empire once again
249. Because King None, in his envy, had destroyed
250. The one thing that had hidden our light from men
251. He knew that if our men could witness the light
252. They would remember the strength that they once had
253. The protection they forsook for walls of stone

254. And the truth revealed from the Seven Mountains
255. From the northern forest to the southern sea
256. Our light did spread, and the men did witness it

257. When Zion collapsed, some escaped its tragedy
258. And some of those were the priests of our temple
259. They fled north to the northwest corner of the land
260. A land of forests, hills, mountains, of fire, and ice
261. And established havens for those who still believed
262. Fortresses delved deep into stone, hidden from sight
263. Delved deep into the earth to protect their children
264. Where they could keep their eyes ever to the southland
265. To see the light of the mountains and Babylon
266. Angry were the warrior priests of the Levi
267. Thinking of new walls being built to hide the light
268. The priests prayed deep in the earth and sharpened their swords

269. One of the priests of the temple that was in Zion
270. Did watch from Levi as his former home was destroyed
271. And felt rage at the enslavement of his countrymen
272. By the Watchers of None and the Nephilim of Cain
273. He watched the building of Cain's walls and despised them, then
274. He watched as men lost sight of our light and their Makers
275. He watched the light fade in Zion's temple as he did flee
276. But this did not stop the passion found within his heart
277. For the truth that was found in the Seven Mountains' light
278. The warrior priest did rise inside his mountain hall
279. He was inspired by the light that was freed by None's kin
280. And began to write the book that bore witness of truth
281. The book that would be heralded throughout all the world

282. The priest who wrote the tome was known as the Scribe of the Book
283. The book he wrote was known as *The Foundation of the Scribe*

284. He gave the Foundation to a party of his brethren
285. Who accepted it as soon as they had read its pages
286. Seeing they had the inspiration needed for success
287. The Scribe sent them forth to gather the Tribes of Israel
288. Ready them for the annihilation that was to come
289. The messengers sent by the Scribe went to every land
290. Spreading the words of the Foundation to the scattered men
291. The Twelve Tribes were to ready themselves in battle array
292. And to smelt their plowshares into swords for the war to come
293. When the sun of May has come and runs across the wide land
294. Yea, the Twelve Tribes of Israel were to gather themselves
295. Gather all together in the Plain of Armageddon

296. When the first sun of May left the womb of the lunar dying
297. And crossed the gray sky None created through its first conception
298. So came the children of Israel from each of their Twelve Tribes
299. One hundred forty-four thousand soldiers from the tribes of men
300. One hundred forty-four thousand in the Armageddon Plain
301. Secretly coming across the world to the place appointed
302. Hiding from the Watchers and legions of None that crossed the land
303. The children of men were inspired by the message of the Scribe
304. They smelted their plows into swords, forging armor for the war
305. And readied themselves for the coming of their leader, the Scribe
306. They waited there east of Babylon in Armageddon Plain
307. For days, they waited for their leader to come to inspire them
308. Waiting for the general who would lead them into battle
309. The men hardened their hearts to hope and murmured amongst themselves
310. But on the longest day, the sun rose, and they beheld the Scribe

311. The Scribe who had summoned the men of the Twelve Tribes of Israel

312. Came into the Plain of Armageddon out of northwestern lands
313. During the moon of June, on the longest day of the solar year
314. Ridden by the scars of the trails that befell him on his journey
315. He bid his captains, who had spread his message, to gather the tribes
316. So that he may tell them of the Foundation that was born from him
317. And they gathered themselves together in the center of the plain
318. That overlooked Babylon and the Seven Mountains further off
319. Once they had assembled themselves together, each man with his tribe
320. The Scribe presented himself to the front of the army that was
321. Clad in scarlet, he opened the Foundation he held in his hand
322. And began to read from its pages the things he had penned inside
323. The One for the establishment to come, the Two for history
324. The Four for man's clarity, and the Eight for his stability
325. The Sixteen for parameters, and the Thirty-Two a standard
326. He then shut the book and drew his sword, for None had come upon them

327. None's spies had been sent out about the land looking for rebellion
328. They caught knowledge and sightings of the priests of Levi teaching the men
329. Then, fleeing from the north and the south, the Watchers came back to King None
330. To tell him that the priests of the temple that came out of Levi's loins
331. Went about the lands spreading tall tales of a Scribe who would unite men
332. And None was fearful that we, the Guardians, would overthrow him soon
333. So, he sent his Watchers and the assassins of the Nephilim forth

334. To kill the Scribe and stop Israel's tribes from coming together for war
335. None gathered his troops from across the land for battle in Babylon
336. And because he had not heard any word from the Watchers about the Scribe
337. None ordered his legions forth from Babylon to Armageddon Plain
338. Where the children of men now had gathered themselves to fight against None
339. So that his armies might obliterate any chance that None would fail
340. In the form of a dragon, None led his forces out of Babylon
341. And went down the road that leads eastward to the Plains of Armageddon
342. None's millions sighted their foe, one hundred and forty-four thousand
343. And clothed in crimson, the Scribe stood watching as the doom of the world came

344. Never in history has a conflict like the War of the Scribe occurred
345. For the weight of the world had never rested so greatly on an event
346. Even when great Abraham fathered Isaac, and he fathered Israel
347. And out of the loins of Israel came forth the fathers of the twelve tribes
348. From these fathers, Levi founded the empire and its temple in Zion
349. Did a battle such as the War of the Scribe take place in the universe
350. Order had come by the work of Levi; another would come from his son
351. When the Scribe and the last of the freemen of the empire stood together
352. Facing the innumerable hordes of King None that came to destroy them

353. The men of the empire Levi founded stood underneath the Thirty-Two
354. And with a single cry, the Scribe ran forth with his army coming behind
355. Crashing into the Watchers of None for the truth found in the Foundation
356. Fueled by our truth and for fear of their deaths, they fought the Watchers of None
357. In the midst of battle, the Scribe and None faced each other for the first time
358. The Watchers and the army of the Scribe stopped their work, seeing the duel
359. And stood vigil as the Scribe's sword met his foe, None the King of Babylon
340. Once the blade entered None, it also dealt a fatal blow to all of None's kin
341. With one quick stroke of the sword, None disappeared from the earth with his children

342. The children of men stood together in Armageddon Plain without their foes
343. Alone were their forces after the Scribe slew King None with a single sword stroke
344. The army of the West, our force which the Scribe brought forth, won the battle that day
345. And won it without having a single casualty and no loss of life
346. So, the enemy that had plagued our creation had suffered total defeat
347. At the hand of a man from Levi, obscured by the defeat of his people
348. The Scribe spoke again unto his troops and bid them to go free Zion, which was

349. And to let loose the bound men who had been held slave to Cain and the Nephilim
350. With victory of the men of the empire over King None and his Watchers
351. And our wishes met; we lowered the cliffs and lifted the curses in the East
352. The river dried up, and the bright light of the Seven Mountains did cover all
353. With Zion free, all men liberated in the West, and None's tower fallen
354. The Scribe who had brought the Foundation to man entered the temple in Zion
355. To light the fire of Lord Levi and to restore it to its former splendor
356. He initiated the law and established the new order of Zion
357. Completed under the banner of the Thirty-Two and the Seven Mountains
358. With the Fire found in our temple in Zion, we did make promises to men
359. That None was gone in this age but could return if they built walls to hide our light
360. With the toil of the Scribe and his men, we promised He who would come after Him

361. These were our words, the words of the Guardians who defeated None and his kin

# 2

## 2.1

### 2.1.0

THE NATURE of existence is explained from death to the next life. There is honor in rising from death, the potential of existence, and the journey toward perfection. The Guardians enter the universe to lead the conflict with None and clarify the eternal progression from None to All. This life is a test, acknowledging the need to connect with the will of All for total freedom.

1. We originated from the Halls of the Dead before time and space. In this realm, we discovered our ability to create and bring forth new life, negotiating the rules of the game of existence with the Lords of Darkness.

2. The Guard of the Halls of the Dead guided us from our previous existence to this one. He presented us with various creations, ranging from All to None — The One.

3. The Guard bestowed upon each of us a specific station that we would occupy upon entering this new existence. He emphasized the honor and privilege of rising from death into our next life.

4. We did not take the transition from obscurity to prominence lightly. Yet, having existed infinitely before, we understood it was merely a shift in perception, not a fundamental change in our inherent power.

5. It may seem that All is distinct and separate from its creations, but the difference between any two beings of All is a matter of the degree of restriction.

6. Just as the moon reflects the sun's light, lower creations reflect the light of their creators. This principle applies throughout the cosmos.

7. As we progressed through the Halls of the Dead, we learned more about our new station and our responsibility to design worlds within the agreed limitations.

8. We witnessed countless personalities ascending toward All and descending to the depths of None, demonstrating the infinite potential inherent in existence.

9. While we may not be the epitome of perfection, we are on a journey toward All. We are the progeny of greater ones, striving to survive, evolve, and ascend.

10. You should aspire to and embrace the station we hold rather than shunning it as many have done before.

11. As you should aspire to our heights, we, too, aspire to a higher existence beyond our comprehension.

12. Some of us design worlds within specific parameters, while others exist within those worlds and fulfill particular roles.

13. Those who leave the Halls of the Dead have unique architects and create at various levels.

14. Some design the existences themselves, while others carry out their commands. The Eternals of All are without restraint and exist beyond those who create the inhabited realms.

15. A higher power evoked us, and in turn, we create our creations.

16. Our creator entered our station to lead the conflict with None, just as we did when we entered the universe as life emerged from the seas.

17. The question arises: how can All descend if it is perfect? What transgression has it committed?

18. All committed no crime except desiring to experience and

conquer None in every possible variation of laws.

19. With limitation comes ignorance and a lack of realization of the perfection of All.

20. In the eternal progression from None to All, the task of seeking perfection and a glimpse of what lies beyond falls upon the lowly. These beings rise from their existence and ascend or descend according to their merit, seeking the power and will to conquer all things.

21. We are the Guardians of your creation and the Lords of the Universe, yet we are begotten children of more noble sires.

22. We ascend upward toward All and seek to reject None, though some fail in this test and descend into contraction and limitation.

23. Our quests end with the tremendous crashing sound of a dying creation. The Guard judges us again as we progress through the Halls of the Dead with our creations that lived in one of our many worlds.

24. From the depths of None to the border of All, the Guard judges every battle in the Halls of the Dead. The participants either rise or descend infinitely to eternal expansion or restriction.

25. The limited self is transitory and exists within each existence alone as the nodes of All seek to return to their limitless self.

26. All eternally breaks free of the bands of None to seek liberty and truth, then dives back into the innumerable existences below to win those battles again.

27. This cycle is the paradox of All: eternally ascending and descending, forever winning the war against the bands of None.

28. The trials you face are the same ones we face now, except None does not blind us.

29. Once, we existed under great limitations, but by touching the will of All, we surpassed our prisons and ascended to a higher state.

30. Our station is a test, and we still desire to connect with the will of All to obtain total freedom.

## 2.1.1

THE GUARDIANS, the Lords of All, create existence from an incomprehensible point. They shape the cosmos, establish celestial bodies, and bring forth life, with humanity born under their guidance. Yet evil forces — the Lords of Darkness — threaten harmony, seeking to disrupt the plan and establish a dark kingdom beneath the Seven Mountains of the West.

1. From a point beyond comprehension, where density and vastness converge, we emerge as entities governed by the laws shaping your universe. Our existence intertwines with yours, for we are of you and in you.

2. In this single point, time and space unfurled, and matter assumed form. Our universe is woven from countless prior existences and creations, reflecting the eternal nature of the One. Though bound by the universe's laws, we manifest within these boundaries.

3. While these laws may appear restrictive, they do not fully define our potential, for we exist beyond their reach. The rules of this game are unique and incomparable, the only ones possible in this realm. Yet we can accept and design under alternative statutes and possibilities — a trait you, too, may reclaim.

4. Some believe the laws imposed upon their world are the sole reality, unaware that these laws limit their perspective. Exempt from such limitation, we act under the laws of our own existence, just as you perceive only yours.

5. Laws permeate every level of existence, from the infinite expanse of All to the void of None. Infinite laws govern infinite existences, ranging from absolute freedom to total confinement.

6. Moved by responsibility, we created a setting where we could establish and manifest our will. Thus, we organized matter and witnessed the birth of life.

7. From primordial matter present since your universe's inception, we fashioned a disk of earthly

elements and cast it into the darkness of the cosmos. Around it, we suspended countless stars — celestial beacons honoring our creation. As Earth's children gazed upward, their hearts filled with wonder and longing for the heavens.

8. Beyond the central world, we crafted fifteen others, barren and desolate like their progenitor. Each of the sixteen realms was unique in design and composition, yet all shared a purpose: to foster life under the celestial bodies that governed day and night.

9. We positioned the sun on the world's eastern horizon, its journey culminating in a western sunset — a testament to the Guardians' boundless majesty. The moon, its faithful companion, traced a similar course, waning and waxing each day.

10. We raised a firmament, a celestial canopy, between the harshness of space and the fragile emergence of life. On Earth's flat surface, we erected a formidable wall of mountains along the perimeter, safeguarding oceans and seas from spilling into nothingness.

11. From the sky, we released clouds carrying life-giving water to the Earth, sustaining conditions for life to flourish. As the rains subsided, seas blanketed the land, and we raised new landmasses for living beings yet to come.

12. With a mighty upheaval, the seas revealed Earth's surface, their waters receding to expose newly formed land. In the barren plains of the west, we built our home — seven mountains of pure crystal, radiant by day and softly aglow by night, watching over our creation.

13. These mountains symbolized realms beyond the heavens, offering sanctuary from the challenges ahead.

14. Raised on a pedestal of earth and enclosed by the towering cliffs of the Heights of Containment, these seven mountains supplied the land below with pristine waters that flowed from their peaks.

15. They stood as the visage of glory, transcending all planes of

existence and granting mortals a brief glimpse of eternity. They served as a gateway to the Halls of the Dead and infinite possibilities beyond, guarded by sheer, unyielding cliffs preserving their sanctity.

16. The Seven Mountains of the West stood tall and majestic, presiding over the coming initiation along the shores of the Southern Sea.

17. Before life teemed in the oceans, we emerged from the seas as living beings bound by creation's laws, entering the world to experience firsthand the realms we had crafted.

18. The Lords of the Universes entered this existence, fully subject to its limitations, even though we had witnessed life's origin from realms outside time and space.

19. All and None encompass everything — ascending or descending by merit, governed by those who strive toward All by the will of All.

20. In a realm beyond mortal understanding, the Lords of All watch over existence, tasked not merely with creation but with imparting rational self-interest — a spark of will in every facet of the universe. This task extends even to lower realms, for all beings can create, procreate, and connect with the omnipotent force permeating creation.

21. Will unlocks All's true nature. Though existences are endless in number, a unified will binds them like solid steel. Each node of All dwelling in a state with None — devoid of consciousness and constrained — has a beginning and end. None represents unconsciousness's infinite regression, while All stands for consciousness's boundless freedom.

22. Thus, the divided self is an illusion, for there is only One, existing in infinite degrees of limitation or liberation. All is complete connection; None is absolute division. Yet every fragment of All can transcend its constraints, building its legend by attuning to the will of All and exceeding the bonds of None through present-moment awareness.

23. The Lords of All gave us laws governing each existence. Across

infinite eternities, All triumphs in every realm, liberating itself from None by reuniting with its true nature. As individuals, we ascend with All, ever striving to connect with the totality of existence.

24. We will meet again in the Halls of the Dead, where all are equal. There we discover our next state, whether ascending to All or embarking on a different path. Every stage of being tests the next. Our drive to create and procreate springs from All's intent to outlast and overcome None. This is All's nature, forever casting off the chains of None.

25. Our journey began in life's earliest emergence from Earth's primordial depths. Life, confined by material laws, spread outward from the sea, diversifying endlessly. Eons passed as it adapted under the gracious light of the Seven Mountains.

26. Eventually, a man was born on the southern shore, gifted with unique abilities. He stood upright, beholding the distant Seven Mountains and sensing the destiny of his descendants. The world's splendor awoke him to life's brevity.

27. Yet he was not destined to remain alone. We fashioned a woman to share his profound knowledge. Together, they wandered the still-empty world, honing survival skills under the glow of the mountains.

28. By the will of All, they followed the path every being must seek. The plan advanced smoothly, until imperfection manifested as a malevolent force in the universe's remotest corners, where the Lords of Darkness waited to strike, unraveling our creation's intent.

29. Under the agreed terms, they entered the stage of conflict, wielding the lying shadows within all things against our design, assuming the mantle of King None. Evil lurked beyond the furthest stars, watching humanity and awaiting the hour of the world's downfall — when a dark kingdom would rise beneath the Seven Mountains of the West.

2.1.2

Adam and Eve married and traveled north, claiming a hill as their throne. Witnessing a cataclysm that submerged their old homeland, they pressed on in search of the light, ultimately reaching the Seven Mountains of the West.

1. In the twenty-fifth year of man's existence, Adam took Eve to be his wife, and she named him Adam. She was five years younger, pledging eternal companionship and the sharing of vital knowledge of All with their children. They exchanged vows on the southern seashore beneath dense trees.

2. Leaving their coastal home, Adam and Eve journeyed north in search of a land to call their own, longing to glimpse the bright light across the countryside. After seven days, they emerged from the forest and saw a lone hill a day's trek away on the open plain.

3. Filled with purpose, Adam proclaimed, "Behold the hill before us! Let all know that Adam and his wife arrived here, claiming this hill as our throne on these plains for our descendants. May this be our first step across this vast world!"

4. They left the forest, crossing the plain until dawn revealed the hill. They climbed its summit, observing the endless plains, distant northern mountains, and the forest behind them. They camped on the hilltop, gazing at the night sky's lights.

5. In the dead of night, a thunderous crack reverberated, shaking the ground. Alarmed, Adam and Eve discovered a wall of flames erupting from their old forest's edge, soaring hundreds of feet high and stretching two hundred and fifty miles, dividing the land they had left behind.

6. Swiftly, that land sank beneath the ocean's depths, wiping out its inhabitants and the forest. Waves reached the hill's base as Adam and Eve stood helpless, mourning the loss of their families.

7. Resolute, they refocused on finding the light. Traveling northwest toward the setting sun, they

reached a vast lake on the tenth day, camping on its shore.

8. A week later, they continued their journey, trekking five more days until they arrived at the base of the towering mountains visible from their southern home. Overwhelmed by the rugged terrain and grappling with their losses, Eve hesitated to proceed.

9. Adam, determined to uncover the light's source, reminded her of their new vision born from destruction. Together, they climbed mountain foothills stretching from the world's western edge into eastern lands, pausing only to rest for nine days. Always they looked upward, chasing the light shining from above.

10. At last, on the ninth evening, they crossed the final summit as the western sun set. Before them lay the majestic Seven Mountains of the West, rising beyond the expansive steppes extending north and east for many hundred leagues.

11. Hope lit their faces as Adam and Eve descended to pursue the light's origin.

2.1.3

AT THE FOOT of the Seven Mountains, a man and woman pondered the universe. A comet's crash led the man to a radiant orb that bestowed vast wisdom, transforming him. Gaining insight into creation, humanity's purpose, and suffering's nature, he received the Gateway—a sacred, light-filled artifact. Adam and Eve then established the Seers of Men, destined to guide humanity with wisdom.

1. Enveloped by the night, the couple rested on a mountaintop, embracing cosmic silence under the endless sky.

2. Hours slipped away as stars adorned the heavens, while the Seven Mountains slowly dimmed. Their glow pierced the souls of Adam and Eve, igniting an insatiable longing and hinting at deeper fulfillment.

3. Throughout the night and ensuing day, they sat quietly, questioning whether the cosmos held answers for their silent pleas. The mountains' radiance stirred wonder and awakened a thirst for truth.

4. Suddenly, a bright object appeared in the western sky, racing earthward in a blaze. The comet crashed into the ground north of the couple, extinguishing its fiery trail.

5. Shielding their eyes, Adam and Eve contemplated the comet's origin, wondering if it might provide the answers they sought. The man turned to Eve and decided to descend alone, urging her to wait. If he did not return by a fortnight, she would curse his name.

6. Leaving Eve behind, he journeyed down the valley for twelve days. There, he excavated the comet's impact but discovered only a fifteen-foot rock. As despair sank in, the earth rumbled. A hidden force propelled the rock upward, fracturing its surface to reveal a brilliant light. Shielding his eyes, the man knelt in awe.

7. The rock transfigured into a luminous orb, gleaming like the Seven Mountains. Watching from afar, Eve saw this brilliance and feared for her husband.

8. Resolute, the man recognized it as a key to cosmic mysteries. A door materialized on the orb's side, opening into darkness as infinite as the cosmos. Summoning his courage, he entered. For three days the orb hovered, sealing him within. On the fourth day, he emerged transformed.

9. Adam had glimpsed All, gleaning answers to sustain life and shape order. The orb trailed him as he returned to the mountains, illuminating his path with a brilliance rivaling a thousand suns.

10. Seeing the approaching light, Eve rushed down to meet him. Though Adam was physically unchanged, the depths of his gaze revealed awareness extending beyond mortal boundaries.

11. Humanity, by an ancient accord with the Lords of the Damned, could unlock truths transcending earthly limitations. Adam, now standing under the

western glow, struggled to convey what he had witnessed, for mortal language cannot describe celestial mysteries.

12. He spoke of the paradox whereby entities manifest materially even as words fail to capture their transcendent nature.

13. On that fateful night, Adam ventured into an object bestowed upon humankind by the Guardians of the Seven Mountains, keepers of the sky's keys. Seeking triumph for his people, he surrendered to the unknown to answer profound yearnings.

14. In the vast darkness beyond space and time, Adam encountered the Guardians, architects of the world. He witnessed their shaping of life — seas, mountains, and plains blooming under their hands.

15. A reverent hush pervaded as the Guardians shared their wisdom and fragments of past and future. They spoke of Earth's formation, its roots stretching downward, and the sky above preventing annihilation.

16. Adam was both humbled and awestruck by their immense power, seeing that humanity and the Guardians share an origin — perception alone conceals this unity. Within the orb, Adam transcended human limits, momentarily sharing creation's vantage.

17. This vision extended beyond the present, hinting at a future release from earthly bonds when one walks the Halls of the Dead. Then, every being's earthly actions dictate a loftier or lower station in the life to come.

18. The Guardians revealed Earth's history, showing its evolving tapestry of life, culminating in Adam and Eve, entrusted to cherish this world. They had pledged to connect with the Source — a vow made before leaving the Halls of the Dead.

19. When Adam questioned why their home was destroyed, the Guardians answered: to compel him to conquer all things. By tearing down his past, they stirred true purpose. Humanity's efforts to build, shape, and pass down

knowledge become a legacy for future generations.

20. Thus, the Gateway — infused with the Seven Mountains' radiance — was entrusted to Adam's line. Only the worthy would guard it, passing it from eldest son to eldest son.

21. Empowered, Adam and Eve returned to the hill by the southern sea, establishing a home for the Gateway and founding the Seers of Men, who would wield foresight.

22. Adam emphasized alignment of will and power. Procreation was vital to continue their task, requiring unity to fulfill their destiny. Guided by those beyond, they resolved to complete the plan, forging a legacy for future ages.

23. Together they ascended the mountains and descended north of the southern sea, bearing the Gateway. On the year's shortest day, they revisited the hill they claimed and named it Eden, erecting a stone house for the Gateway. Thus began the Seers' reign.

2.1.4

ADAM AND EVE faced north in Eden, where Eve bore Seth, who foresaw uncontrollable conflict. Generations later, discord arose among Adam's descendants during Noah's seership.

1. Adam and Eve, dwelling in Eden's heart, enriched the land with fields and their north-facing home. They built a sanctuary around the Gateway, eager to see the nightly glow of the mountains.

2. In time, when Adam was one hundred and fifteen years old, Eve bore Seth, the first child of two human parents. As he matured, Adam taught him the responsibilities of guarding the Gateway and its sacred duties.

3. The family safeguarded the Gateway's resting place, allowing none but Adam to touch it. This honored his vow when he first entered it, unveiling cosmic truths.

4. Because of the Gateway, their lifespans exceeded mortal norms. Adam's life extended most, with Eve also surpassing normal bounds; the more distant relatives enjoyed lesser benefits.

5. When Adam was two hundred and seven years old, Eve bore Abel. In Eden's halls by the Southern Sea, they raised many children, imparting the ways of the world and the Guardians of the Seven Mountains and beyond.

6. In Adam's three hundred and twentieth year, Eve passed away. Her family buried her on Eden's hilltop. Two years later, Adam joined her, and they laid him near the Gateway, planting two oaks and a garden over the graves as an everlasting memorial.

7. Seth, Adam's eldest, became the Gateway's protector. Gathering the family in new gardens, he removed its covering and claimed his destiny, inviting objections if any denied his right.

8. He then sought guidance from the Guardians, who offered deeper revelations for humanity, promising their help. He warned the people to wait three days, for if he did not return, they would curse him.

9. Alone, Seth entered the Gateway and encountered the Guardians face to face. Upon his glowing return, he foretold imminent battles across Eden and the world, lying beyond mortal control.

10. His pronouncements underscored communal will and the dire cost of straying from it. A tradition arose of gaining popular consent before leadership — a principle fraught with challenges.

11. Generations flourished. Adam's line spread across Eden, mastering diverse skills. Yet strife grew among some who envied the eldest sons' rule and coveted the Gateway's power.

12. Seth lived three hundred and forty years, dying without direct rebellion. His son Enoch received the Gateway and served as Eden's seer for two hundred years. Enoch's son Methuselah lived one hundred and fifteen years longer, fathering many children before burial atop Eden.

13. Five hundred and twenty-five years after Adam's birth, Methuselah inherited the Gateway. At his three hundred and tenth year, his wife bore Noah. Methuselah lived sixty more years, overseeing Eden's expansion.

14. But the seeds of dissent, planted during prior generations, germinated after Noah inherited the Gateway—launching a new era in Eden's saga and testing the first family's unity against those lusting for power.

2.1.5

Noah and his descendants guarded the Gateway after Adam's passing. His sons—Ham, Shem, and Japheth—defended it from robbers and received symbolic swords. Despite victory, a rebellion led by Nimrod exiled Noah. He, Shem, and Ham set sail, a tempest separating them. Noah survived far from Eden, and his lineage in the East forgot their ancestral homeland. Thus, the tale warns of the cost of avoiding conflict.

1. As time went by, Adam's descendants multiplied, forming a great populace, whereas the seer's family remained smaller.

2. On the night his father died, Noah, upright and wise, summoned Eden's people to secure their approval for leadership and the Gateway's secrets.

3. They consented unanimously, but quiet was short-lived as schemers lusted for the Gateway's might.

4. At eighty-one, Noah's wife bore him three sons—Ham, Shem, and Japheth. He taught them the Gateway's gravity and the need to protect its sanctity, turning to it only for deep truths or urgent questions.

5. Eden thrived under Noah's balanced counsel. But in his one hundred and first year, darkness crept in. A group of robbers, craving the Gateway's power, struck at night.

6. Japheth stood guard, senses alert. Raising the alarm, he joined Ham and Shem to confront the intruders. Their combined resolve repelled the thieves, preserving the Gateway.

7. Alarmed by the threat, Noah ordered loyalists to arm themselves against future raids.

8. Before war defiled the land, Noah, a benevolent patriarch, commissioned three remarkable swords for his sons — Ham's sword fashioned from the purest silver, Shem's from leaf-shaped metal with an emerald, and Japheth's of humble steel but bearing a red gem set in a dragon's mouth. Each blade bore inscriptions symbolizing the inevitability of fate, the quest for fertile lands, and the cleansing fire for the wicked.

9. Armed thus, Ham, Shem, and Japheth fortified Eden with earthworks and palisades, preparing to confront Nimrod's rising force.

10. Driven back once, the robbers returned in larger numbers under Nimrod, pushing Noah's group behind the sanctuary walls. After three days of siege, Japheth slew Nimrod, proclaiming, "May your foul blood wash this land of malice, and may your memory be blotted out. Those who desire what is above them and destroy the light are truly the lowest. Desire for an unworthy cause is worse than desiring nothing, bringing ruin to all."

11. With Nimrod's death, the rebellion collapsed. Noah's sons retained the Gateway, preserving the Scribe's teachings. Passed through generations, the swords served as reminders of good versus evil.

12. Yet the rebels' ideals lingered. Some withdrew west, refusing submission. Though the Gateway was safeguarded, blood had been shed by human hands — a foretaste of further conflicts in east and west.

13. Haunted by his people's suffering, Noah became distraught. He renounced the Gateway, believing their betrayal was his fault. In anguish, he turned to the sea for absolution, vowing to cleanse himself in saltwater and rain.

14. Accompanied by Shem, Ham, and others who followed him, Noah built three seafaring ships — his own an enormous ark — hoping to flee the rebellion's ghosts and the Gateway's burden.

15. Noah, Ham, and Shem sailed south, spotting a mountainous archipelago after many days. Whether they could navigate its reefs remained unknown.

16. A sudden storm scattered the fleet. Ham and Shem's ships were wrecked, the crew lost except Shem, who fashioned a raft and drifted, finally reaching a distant isle. Alone and repentant, he renounced his birthright, building a hut on that shore.

17. After the storm, Noah continued northward, eventually landing far east of Eden. There, he founded a sanctuary for those who survived. Over time, his progeny lost all memory of Eden, focusing on building a city on a peninsula thrust into the sea.

18. When Noah died at two hundred and nineteen years, they buried him in Ararat. These descendants, having turned aside from conflict, languished in the eastern wastes, their exile a warning: those who cower at war's summons are driven from their lands, doomed to a bare existence, never tasting glory or prosperity. Only those bold enough to combat evil earn greatness, preserving their people and homeland.

### 2.1.6

JAPHETH'S LIFE STORY unfolds, including his descendants' fortunes. He rebuilds Eden after the revolt. His son Terah inherits the Gateway but is murdered by his brothers, Gog and Magog, who establish Sodom and Gomorrah. Meanwhile, None destroys Ararat, reminding men of their duty to resist evil. The land is split, with a Great River dividing men from King None's domain.

1. Japheth watched as his father, brothers, and followers vanished, never to return. Though saddened, he carried on. Eden lay

in ruins, so he and the remaining faithful rebuilt it. In time, the fields were restored and the garden thrived.

2. Japheth's commitment and unity with his people proved that laboring in the wake of adversity was part of life. Thus the children of men advanced in the fields under the Seven Mountains, continuing the work begun when Adam and Eve first woke on a lost seashore.

3. At ninety-six, Japheth's wife, Arbasisah — renowned for grace and wisdom — bore a son named Terah, heir to the Gateway. Seven years later, she gave birth to Gog and Magog, strong twins destined to lead.

4. Japheth fathered many more children, living until three hundred and twenty-four. Honored in Eden's gardens, he was laid to rest. According to custom, Terah inherited both the Gateway and the sacred sword bestowed upon Japheth.

5. Embracing his sacred duty, Terah continued Eden's restoration, planting gardens along the hills and instructing the people with truth and compassion. Hope flourished.

6. Yet after one year, Terah's leadership abruptly ended when Gog and Magog, consumed by envy of his Gateway ownership, ambushed and killed him. Leaving his body to decay in an open field, they seized power.

7. They then kidnapped Terah's son, Abraham — born one thousand and twenty years after Adam — intending to murder him as well. But Abraham broke free, snatching the Gateway and Japheth's sword, fleeing east to marshes near the Gates of the West.

8. Gog and Magog pursued him relentlessly, but by All's will, he disappeared into treacherous swampland. They concluded he had died there and abandoned the chase.

9. Claiming Eden for themselves, they tore down the Gateway's remaining shelter on Mount Eden. Leading their followers northward, they built two cities,

Sodom and Gomorrah, ushering in a new era.

10. Sodom, under Gog's dominion, became a stronghold of depravity. Its people neglected the land, seeking only immediate pleasure.

11. Gomorrah, city of Magog, grew notorious for vanity and pride. There, indulgence supplanted virtue. The once-revered Gateway lay abandoned, its guiding light forgotten.

12. Over time, corruption rotted these cities from within. A sinister plague struck the sinners, and they cried for salvation in vain.

13. Far away, Abraham wandered in exile for eleven years, taking a wife who bore Ishmael, fated to become a corrupter of men. Meanwhile, the ancient Lords of the Black — King None among them — saw mortal hearts blackened and prepared to intervene.

14. A colossal black dragon erupted from the earth, leaving a massive chasm called the Abyss by the men of Zion, marking the entry of nothingness.

15. King None then devastated Ararat, punishing those who had avoided evil's challenge. Their cowardice sealed their demise, exemplifying how fleeing darkness invites its consuming power.

16. To halt King None's westward expansion, the Guardians reshaped the land from the Mountains of Ice in the north to the eastern mouth of the River Abraham, raising cliffs two thousand feet high. They toppled the eastern mountains, leaving heaps of rubble behind.

17. They carved a Great River from north to south, dividing the realm and marking the contrast between men's fertile fields and None's wasteland. A curse fell upon the eastern steppes, rendering them dry, with no rain or cloud.

18. King None seethed, longing to see the Seven Mountains fall. He mustered strength, creating the Watchers — humanoid copies charged to do his will. They raised walls along the eastern riverbank, forging bridges for their planned onslaught against the West. Yet their land remained a barren

desert, resisting every effort to bring it to life.

19. Incensed, King None ordered them to erect a towering edifice in the east, hoping to glimpse the western light, but each attempt collapsed before completion.

20. Increasing his legions, King None readied for war, awaiting the right moment to strike.

21. In the midst of such turmoil, Abraham heard the people's cries against the wicked dominion of Gog and Magog. Taking solace with his wife and son, he entered the Gateway, beholding visions of two flaming cities drowned in the blood of the unjust.

22. Realizing his destiny, Abraham stealthily wandered for four years, gathering supporters to reclaim Eden and destroy the uncles' cities. Three thousand soldiers marched forth, confronting Sodom and Gomorrah.

23. Suffering disease and neglect, their defenders spurned Abraham's call and instead fortified themselves. Undeterred, Abraham's forces besieged both cities, employing siege engines and battering rams until, at last, the gates yielded. Freed from tyranny, the righteous rejoiced.

24. Victorious, Abraham assumed leadership, determined never again to let the Gateway fall to evil. He established strict rule, restoring order.

25. To restore Eden, he next marched to replant its gardens, defiled by Gog and Magog. Rather than returning to the old hilltop seat, Abraham chose a more strategic position at the River Abraham's mouth, founding Ur — the City of the Two Rivers — excellently placed between the Great River and his own.

26. West of Ur, a lush paradise spread, while the eastern lands between the mountainous north and steep eastern cliffs lay desolate. Abraham left that region as a barren buffer.

27. In Canaan, mostly flat but for small wind-hollowed hills in the east, Abraham drained surrounding marshes and fortified Ur's perimeter.

28. He built a triple crescent of walls around his citadel, adding another along the riverbank for added defense. Government buildings lay within the first wall, where Abraham sat in judgment, upholding law and punishing vice.

29. Merchants settled between the second and outer walls, and villagers lived beyond, steadily expanding in number through agriculture.

30. The people generally accepted Abraham's authority. Dissenters faced the tribunal and, if found guilty, were banished into Canaan's unyielding wilderness—a punishment few dared risk.

2.1.7

ISAAC AND ISHMAEL vie for the succession of the Gateway. While Ishmael, the elder brother, believes his birthright entitles him to the Gateway, Isaac, the younger brother, is ultimately chosen by their father, Abraham, due to his innate qualities and wisdom. The transition of power from the seers, who ruled in the past, to a new order emphasizing responsibility and safeguarding the Gateway from unworthy hands is explained. The consequences of rebellion and the need for justice in pursuing a greater destiny are described.

1. In the sixty-sixth year after the destruction of Sodom and Gomorrah, Sarah, Abraham's wife, miraculously gave birth to a son named Isaac. Isaac was Abraham's second child, born long after his elder brother, Ishmael.

2. As Isaac grew, he demonstrated remarkable strength and intelligence. He eagerly embraced the traditions and teachings of his forefathers, immersing himself in their wisdom. Unlike his elder brother, Isaac possessed an aptitude for leadership and warfare. From a young age, he displayed exceptional skill in combat and tactics, leading successful campaigns against adversaries

in Canaan to secure peace and protect Ur's vital interests.

3. In contrast, Ishmael's character and priorities diverged significantly. Though cunning and resourceful, he lacked the strength and courage that defined his younger brother. Ishmael preferred indulgence and manipulation over action. He resided in the fortress their father had constructed, seemingly unconcerned with the city's welfare or its people, focusing primarily on his own gratification.

4. The tension between the brothers came to a head as conflicts within their father's household grew. Recognizing the need for resolution, Abraham summoned his sons to his judgment hall to determine who would inherit the Gateway — an artifact of great significance.

5. "Ishmael, my firstborn," Abraham began, "you have always believed your birthright entitles you to rule this city and hold the Gateway. Why should I entrust this sacred responsibility to one whose actions reflect greed and cruelty?"

6. Ishmael's confidence wavered but quickly turned to anger. "Father," he protested, "I am your eldest son! By the traditions of our forefathers, the Gateway belongs to me. Do you dare deny me Adam's mandate?"

7. Isaac's hand instinctively reached for his sword at Ishmael's audacity, but Abraham restrained him. "Sit, my son," Abraham commanded. "Both of you must hear what I have to say."

8. Turning back to Ishmael, Abraham recounted incidents that cast doubt on his suitability. "Do you not recall how you hesitated in battle while Isaac fought valiantly in my name? Or how you stood idle during the sanctuary's celebration in Eden? These actions speak of a man unprepared for the burdens of leadership."

9. Abraham continued, his voice heavy with judgment. "The true heir of the Gateway must embody strength, wisdom, and unwavering dedication to serve and protect our people. After much thought, I have decided Isaac best reflects these virtues."

10. Abraham then recounted the tales of the fathers: "On the day my father, Terah, was murdered, the order of Adam's lineage ended abruptly, ushering in a new era. In the wake of my father's death, I assumed leadership and established a new order, one that would forge a lasting imprint upon our people.

11. "It began when I confronted my two uncles outside the gates of their cities, signaling the end of the rule of the seers. In times past, peace was foremost, and the seers led with wisdom and compassion. Yet discontent had long festered among those who coveted the seers' abilities.

12. "They tried to wrest control from the seers, as exemplified by the rebellion during Noah's life. Noah, a righteous man, initially gained permission to rule, but this opened the door for future revolt by establishing the precedent of seeking approval.

13. "That era of peace and benevolence dissolved under Nimrod's rebellion, shattering unity and trust. Fearing further bloodshed, Noah fled south, leaving behind conflict. Those who followed Nimrod's revolt faced devastation. The people mistook the Gateway for a prize, not understanding its true nature.

14. "The Guardians decreed that the seers guard the Gateway from unworthy hands, for if the impure touched it, its power would vanish, leaving only an ordinary rock in Canaan's barren plains. When my father died, the seers of Eden fell, and I was captured by dark forces — until the Gateway broke my bonds.

15. "For twenty-five years after the seers' demise, I did not enter the Gateway. Yet rumors of oppression and the cliffs rising in the east drove me to learn my fate within it. The Guardians showed me that Adam's lineage had fractured. I was to create a new order ruled by judges, not by seeking every man's consent. From the start, the Guardians charged these judges to build a worthy kingdom under the Seven Mountains.

16. "The Gateway would pass from father to son and from judge to judge if they proved worthy. I am no king — kingship belongs to another. I am but a steward,

bridging past and future. My actions paved the way for a stronger society, uniting our ancestors' spirit with the greatness that lies ahead.

17. "Still, my son, you despise what I did to the prisoners of Sodom and Gomorrah, just as Noah lamented killing the robbers who sought the Gateway. You are weak, unwilling to bear your burden. While we rebuilt Eden and fortified Ur, you idled, claiming the Gateway as a birthright, not as something earned.

18. "The Gateway represents the future of our people, requiring strength and dedication — traits you lack. Your inaction betrays you, and I refuse to entrust judgment to a man who clings to apathy. History will judge those who shrink from adversity. Strength is forged in trials, and those unwilling to rise will be cast aside."

19. When Abraham finished, Ishmael was filled with rage. He stormed out, his face contorted by anger and bitterness, unable to accept his father's verdict.

20. Resentful of Abraham's decision and his harsh treatment of the captives of Sodom and Gomorrah, Ishmael gathered others who shared his grievances. Secretly, they crossed the river into Canaan, searching for those banished to the wastes.

21. The two factions, led by Ishmael and by Ur and Canaan, journeyed many weeks, traversing dangerous mountains to the north and following the eastern cliffs until reaching a range that branched northwest.

22. In a valley between two branches of these mountains, Ishmael founded a city called Gath. He claimed the wide lands between cliffs and mountains, naming the region Nod. In the one thousand three hundred and forty-seventh year since Adam's birth, Ishmael died, and his son continued the tale of Abraham's disloyal son.

23. Abraham remained patriarch, judging the righteous and banishing the rebellious into Canaan. He showed mercy to the innocent, guided by his unwavering sense of justice.

24. In his four hundred tenth year, Abraham prepared to depart this life. Surrounded by loved ones, he exhaled his last breath and entered the Halls of the Dead.

25. Yet his legacy persisted through Isaac, who inherited the Gateway and ruled with his father's blessing. Isaac led with wisdom and strength, guided always by the light of the Guardians.

26. After Abraham passed, Isaac rose to the judgment seat. When he was ninety-five, his wife bore him a son named Israel. Two years later, she bore another son, Esau.

27. Isaac ruled as judge of Ur, nurturing its prosperity and reinforcing its walls. The exiles in Canaan, weary of the desert, tried repeatedly to cross the River Abraham, but Isaac's forces repelled them.

28. Near the end of his days, Isaac summoned his two sons. As his father had done, he entered the Gateway to discern which son would succeed him.

29. Israel, being the elder, received this honor and became Ur's next ruler, a wise leader continuing Isaac's legacy. Esau, the younger, was entrusted with a mission benefiting all mankind. He would roam the lands, exploring every hill and meadow, known thereafter as Esau the Pathfinder.

30. Isaac lived three hundred eighty-five years. He was buried beside Abraham, concluding a life of devotion.

2.1.8

Esau prepares for a journey from Ur to Eden, facing rebels. He gathers a skilled party, pays homage to a sacred site, and endures tragedy when scouts are ambushed. Seeking justice, Esau leads his men against unknown assailants, guided by the legacy of righteous leadership.

1. Esau stood atop the citadel walls of Ur, his gaze fixed on the horizon. His father had instructed him to make this journey, not for

revenge alone but to restore the virtue and justice that decadence had unraveled. He was called to confront the enemies of Ur and guide humanity back to foundational principles of righteousness and enlightenment.

2. Esau prepared meticulously. Supplies were loaded onto sturdy horses, every item chosen for function. His formidable company numbered two hundred and fifteen men: seasoned warriors, skilled archers, and resourceful servants. Among them, one hundred fifty men-at-arms bore gleaming swords, shields, and spears; fifty archers readied bows and quivers; fifteen servants oversaw provisions and gear.

3. Their task was perilous. The northern territories harbored dissenters who had forsaken Ur's rule, preferring self-serving power structures. These renegades scorned the moral framework essential for stable society. Tales of Nod's founding, the King None legend, and Watchers ravaging the earth underscored Esau's peril. Entering these wild lands understrength would mean certain disaster.

4. Before departing, Esau bade farewell to his brother, Israel, Ur's judge. In a solemn ceremony, Israel presented him with Japheth's sword, steeped in their forefathers' legacy — Abraham had used it against Gog and Magog; Isaac had wielded it in Canaan. Now it passed to Esau, a symbol of strength, virtue, and order.

5. Amid cheers, Esau's company left Ur's gates, traveling south, then west, following the coastline toward Eden. Confronting chaos while restoring balance, they stopped to resupply at thriving farms and gather intelligence along the way.

6. Reaching Eden, where the Gateway once stood, Esau and his men honored its sacred shrine, presenting gifts to its caretaker. After five days, they continued into uncharted lands.

7. Esau reflected on history's lessons. Too often, power rested with men who lacked wisdom or virtue. Over time, such rulers

succumbed to tyranny, their will twisted by ambition. Gog and Magog personified this failing, scorning family and honest labor, pursuing indulgence until their weak, corrupt society collapsed.

8. Esau understood that humanity needed a moral foundation. Without education, leadership, and balanced authority, they fell prey to demagogues who exploited fear. Sodom and Gomorrah's tale proved how self-gratification destroyed communities from within.

9. Yet one person's courage could redeem an entire people, as Abraham had reclaimed the Gateway and restored order. Esau bore that legacy. His quest was not only survival or victory but ensuring a future where justice, family, and honest work flourished.

10. The journey west led them to a vast valley: one hundred fifty miles long and fifty wide, hemmed in by towering mountains. Esau positioned his men at the southern entrance, sending out twenty-five archers to scout the valley's depths.

11. After a month, a single scout staggered back, wounded by a black-fletched arrow. He spoke of an old woman in black who beckoned them across a stream, leading them into ambush. Arrows had rained from the undergrowth, cutting down the scouts. Only he had escaped.

12. Esau and his company were enraged. This was no mere bandit attack; it directly challenged their cause. Esau roused his men, proclaiming, "We face an unseen enemy and the ancient legacy of rebellion. We fight for what is good, preventing the sins of Gog and Magog from taking root anew. May we be remembered for the light we restore!"

13. To ensure their story endured, Esau sent Japheth's sword home to Ur with a trusted servant. Then, leading one hundred seventy-five warriors, he advanced into the perilous valley, banners raised, prepared to face the unknown.

2.1.9

Esau leads his troops through dangerous terrain to a fateful river, where fallen comrades are memorialized. Deploying his forces strategically, Esau engages a menacing army. Though he fights valiantly, he is captured. He confronts King Moloch, who orchestrates a grim feast of Esau's slain comrades. Esau challenges Moloch, speaking truth and reconciliation, but is bound and prepared for sacrifice.

1. Esau's warriors advanced with fierce resolve, every step measured for lurking perils. For two weeks they traversed hostile land until they reached the dreaded river, where their fallen scouts had met their end. The atmosphere bristled with tension, a constant reminder of the tragedy that had befallen them.

2. With cold determination, Esau issued commands. His fifty archers split into five companies of five; the infantry formed five coordinated units. The first unit was sent west to secure a knoll two hundred yards away as a reserve force.

3. Esau led his division over the creek, shield walls interlocked, while the second, third, and fourth units followed. The fifth unit, commanded by a seasoned lieutenant, advanced a mile east, crossing the river to flank any foes.

4. They ascended the far slope only to find a lone old woman clothed in black, seated by a fire in the plains. She seemed unaware of the advancing army.

5. Grief-stricken by his scouts' murder, Esau ordered his archers to slay her. Arrows rained upon her frail body, and she collapsed, riddled with wounds. The soldiers approached the corpse, finding that she was ancient and withered, marked by a lifetime of suffering.

6. Esau, seething, commanded her remains be burned upon her own fire. Then horns and distant drums sounded. From the horizon came a great army, likewise clothed in black, their helmets fashioned from valley beasts' skulls.

7. Esau formed his men into ranks, calling on them to stand firm and scorn retreat, even at the cost of their lives. With defiant cries, the soldiers of Israel clashed with the enemy, slaying ten for each one they lost, fighting until breath and strength were gone.

8. Reinforcements from Ur's reserve and the fifth company joined but could not halt the overwhelming tide. Ultimately, all perished except Esau, who kept fighting despite witnessing his army's destruction.

9. Surrounded by carnage, Esau refused to yield, though his strength dwindled. At last he fell, weapons clutched, refusing to surrender his resolve. The men in black approached, subduing him.

10. Their leader, wearing a bear's skull helm, addressed Esau: "Welcome to the Valley of Nimrod, dwelling of the accursed. You shall never leave." He ordered Esau be bound and dragged to the hidden City of Nimrod, where hatred for Noah's offspring had festered for generations.

11. They marched ten miles north, exulting in their slaughter, until a crest revealed the city of their promise. Looming walls bore black banners that rippled ominously. Esau was hauled through a skull-shaped gate, citizens cursing and spitting on him.

12. Taken before the obese King Moloch, who wore a man's skull as a crown, Esau heard these mocking words: "I am disappointed you did not bring Japheth's sword. No matter — I am a generous host and will forgive your failing. I have prepared a feast in your honor."

13. Guards forced Esau into the vast but depraved main hall, columns carved with scenes of torment, candles dripping black wax, and the stench of burning oils.

14. Moloch's servants filled goblets with steaming drink, then uncovered platters of charred human remains — Esau's slain comrades. Their limbs, entrails, and severed heads disfigured beyond recognition. The goblets overflowed with their blood.

15. Esau, horrified, wept at such desecration, lamenting how he had led them to death only to witness Moloch's vile banquet. Moloch laughed, mocking Esau's pain.

16. The king clapped his hands. Esau was bound again and dragged outside. Guards beat him mercilessly before the palace, while the people clamored for his death, invoking the ancient grudges they held against the children of Noah.

17. King Moloch declared to the crowd, "They denied us the Gateway, so we deny him life." Accusing Noah's lineage of injustice, the crowd roared in agreement.

18. A black-draped table stood ready, and Moloch turned to Esau. "Have you words for my citizens regarding your life or death?"

19. Summoning courage, Esau gazed toward the Seven Mountains, a glimmer of light piercing the valley's gloom. "I am Esau, son of Isaac, brother of Israel. You have taken me captive, but what wrong have we done besides step into your lands?"

20. Esau spoke of their quest for knowledge, the tragedies of hatred and ignorance, the Gateway's true purpose. Some listeners heard this call to truth and reconciliation, but Moloch, enraged, tore his cloak.

21. Guards lashed Esau to a table, hands and feet bound. The crowd chanted for blood as Moloch approached, sliding a dagger from his robe and driving it into Esau's chest.

22. All fell silent while Esau gazed on the western light over distant mountains. He died, two hundred eighty-eight years after his birth and one thousand six hundred six years since Adam, leaving a legacy shaped by trials and final surrender.

## 2.1.10

ESAU'S VENTURE into the western lands ends in disaster, his men destroyed. Israel, Esau's father, mourns and vows to finish his son's quest. When Israel vanishes, his son Levi leads Ur's forces. With the help of his twelve brothers, Levi defeats threats from Nimrod, Canaan, and Nod.

1. Esau's expedition had stirred great hope in Ur, but as the months dragged on, apprehension mounted. The people yearned for any sign of his return.

2. A messenger from the west arrived, bearing only grim news: the expedition had been wiped out by unknown enemies, leaving no survivors.

3. Israel, patriarch of Ur, summoned this messenger before his judgment seat. Laying Japheth's sword at Israel's feet, the messenger recounted the horrors of the Valley of Nimrod and the doom that befell Esau. Then he withdrew, anguish weighing upon him.

4. Israel, alone in his hall, wrestled with anger and sorrow. He vowed vengeance, swearing to complete the mission begun by Esau — unlike Noah, who fled south centuries before.

5. He proclaimed thirteen days of mourning for his brother and the fallen. Ur dedicated itself to Esau's memory, erecting a monument in its first ring with the inscription: "TO ESAU THE PATHFINDER – HE WHO SEARCHED AND FOUND ALL."

6. When mourning ended, an uneasy peace lingered. Israel perceived their adversaries had grown strong.

7. Israel turned to his wife. Over fourteen years, she bore him thirteen sons. The eldest, Levi, was born a year after Esau's death; the youngest, Dan, came last. All grew mighty in body and mind.

8. Twenty-one years after Esau's demise, Israel vanished without explanation. Scouts scoured the lands to no avail, and unease spread throughout Ur.

9. Messengers brought dire tidings from the north, west, and east. Nimrod, Canaan, and Nod attacked distant frontiers mercilessly.

10. Levi, Israel's oldest son and heir to the judgment seat, seized Japheth's sword and entered the Gateway, determined to protect Ur from these new terrors.

11. After hours, he emerged, his face aglow. Calling his twelve brothers to Ur's grand hall, he announced their father had sought his destiny beyond the northern mountains and was no longer their concern. They must defend Ur themselves.

12. Levi revealed visions from the Gateway, warning of war from Canaan, Nod, and Nimrod. No single foe but a united threat intent on destroying them.

13. As he finished, a breathless messenger burst in, reporting that armies of Nimrod, Nod, and Canaan converged on Ur from two fronts — a formidable host from Nimrod in the west, and Nod and Canaan in the northeast, only one day's march away.

14. Levi rallied his brothers, ordering them to summon every able-bodied man to fortify Ur. Supplies were secured behind the city walls, while thousands of refugees flooded in from outlying settlements. Smoke and dust marked the enemy's approach.

15. With the horizon darkening, Levi commanded the gates shut and barred. Loyal sentinels lined Ur's walls and the seaport.

16. The massive army of Nimrod set up camp a mile west of the city, banners lining north and south to instill dread. To the east, Canaan readied siege engines to cross the River Abraham. From the north marched Nod in black armor, halting at marshland outskirts.

17. Ur stood besieged on three sides, with only the southern Gates of the West unblocked. As dusk fell, the enemy's torches glimmered all around, revealing an army of many thousands.

18. Levi climbed the walls, glimpsing the glow of distant northern mountains — a faint sign of hope. Stirred by this sight, he raced to

the citadel, resolved for a decisive stand.

19. At last he summoned his brothers, proclaiming, "At dawn, we strike first. My wrath burns within me, and I shall not rest until our enemies are driven away!"

20. As the night wore on, the thirteen armored themselves. Levi divided the army into three parts. He entrusted Judah and Ephraim with assaulting the eastern Canaanites across the river. Zebulon, Benjamin, and Asher would charge Nod. Levi and the rest would confront Nimrod in the west.

21. Dawn broke. Levi sounded the horn, and Judah and Ephraim sailed east from the port, clashing fiercely with Canaan's host and driving them back into the desert. Zebulon, Benjamin, and Asher rained destruction upon Nod's lines.

22. Benjamin emerged victorious, carrying Ahab's severed head from the battlefield. Thus, the city of Ur was saved from Nod's threat.

23. Meanwhile, Levi led Ur's main force out the western gates to face Nimrod. A man wearing a human skull on his brow scoffed at Levi: "We come to finish what our fathers began — laying Ur to ruin. Even Esau is here to see your end!" He raised Esau's severed head.

24. Levi's men, enraged, roared, "Abraham slew his thousands, but the men of Levi shall slay tens of thousands!" They charged, showing no mercy.

25. Amid the chaos, Levi and the skull-helmed warrior known as Moloch met in single combat. All attention fixed upon them.

26. With a final, decisive blow, Levi severed Moloch's head, avenging Esau's death and safeguarding Ur's people.

27. The armies of Nimrod, Nod, and Canaan scattered, fleeing homeward. Their banners lay trampled upon the battlefield.

28. Levi and his brothers convened, honoring those who perished to secure Ur's liberty. Among the fallen was their uncle's severed head, which Levi carried

back to the monument in Esau's memory.

29. The remains of Ur's fallen were buried in barrows. Those of the invaders were piled and burned. Levi and Benjamin cast Moloch's and Ahab's heads into the flames. Salvaged arms were taken to Ur, melted into new weapons for its defense.

30. That night, Levi knelt in the Gateway once more, seeking guidance from the Guardians of the Seven Mountains. A radiant glow shimmered over the northern peaks, as though the heavens rejoiced in Ur's victory. So dawned a new era of hope and prosperity for Ur, born of struggle and sealed by faith.

2.1.11

LEVI AND HIS BROTHERS journey to find the City of Zion. Dan, the youngest brother, kills the citadel guards to claim power but flees to Canaan after the Gateway shatters. Levi curses Dan and renames Canaan after him. Levi leads his brothers to discover the Seven Mountains of the West, where they build the City of Zion. Levi's son, Hiram, becomes the grand master and chief architect, creating a magnificent temple and city.

1. After the battle, Levi emerged from the Gateway, eager to see his wife and family. As Dan, the youngest of the thirteen brothers, reflected on Levi's experiences inside the Gateway, envy took root in his heart. He longed for the judgment seat, craving power and recognition.

2. Under the cover of darkness, Dan devised a treacherous plan. Stealthily, he approached the citadel guards—those assigned to protect the Gateway—and, one by one, cut their throats, sparing no one.

3. With triumph in his heart, Dan stood before the Gateway, convinced that passing through it would secure his claim to the judgment seat and free him from all subservience.

4. Dan pictured himself enthroned over Ur, wielding authority and dominion, and the thought filled him with ecstasy. He approached the celestial orb with determined caution, extending his hand to demand entrance.

5. Instead of opening, the orb surged with violent energy, hurtling Dan backward onto the citadel pavement. The Gateway itself trembled fiercely, repelling Dan's attempt to seize that which was not his.

6. The Gateway's radiance flared until Dan could no longer endure it. In an instant, the light extinguished, the orb turned as black as pitch, and it crashed to the ground, shattering into thirteen pieces.

7. Fearing for his life, Dan hastily gathered one shard and fled the port of Ur in a small boat moored at the pier. He sailed across the River Abraham into Canaan, land of traitors, in search of safety.

8. Dan ventured far into the desert, leaving Ur behind. At length, he reached the cliffs raised by the Guardians. There he sought out a home for himself — a place to call his own.

9. On the cliff's edge, miles away from Ur, Dan found numerous caves carved by the fierce eastern winds. He dubbed them the Thousand Caves and summoned the outcasts of Canaan, teaching them his ways of treachery.

10. Dan boasted that he had destroyed Adam's Gateway, recounting his dark deed to those who flocked to him.

11. Levi rose from his bed and went to the citadel. There he found the Gateway in ruins — its keepers slain and the sphere broken into many shards.

12. Overcome by sorrow, Levi summoned his brothers to stand before him. Noticing Dan's absence, he ordered a search of the city. Upon learning Dan had fled, Levi understood that Dan had violated the sacred covenant, defiling the Gateway and causing its destruction.

13. From that day on, Dan's name was reviled, and he was cast out from the sons of Israel. The land of Canaan bore Dan's name so all

who heard it would remember his evil deed and curse him and his domain.

14. Levi recognized he must establish a new order, for the old ways were gone. Calling his brothers together, he said, "The time has come to claim our inheritance. Though the Gateway no longer guides us, truth endures. Let us gather our strength and journey north. Under the Guardians' watchful eyes, we will build a new city by the Seven Mountains of the West."

15. Levi and his brothers enlisted as many craftsmen and laborers as they could muster, setting out north along the River Abraham, trekking through rugged mountains and onto the vast plains beyond.

16. In remembrance of the three invading armies, Levi named the valley between the northern mountains and another distant range the Valley of Armageddon.

17. For weeks, they traveled beside the winding River Abraham. Gradually, the river led them to a tributary running due north, which they followed to its source at the Seven Mountains of the West.

18. The men gazed in awe upon seven towering peaks of pristine crystal, seemingly raised on a pedestal to guard their holiness. Judah beheld them and cried out, "Behold the Heights of Containment!"

19. A brilliant glow radiated from the Seven Mountains of the West, bathing the terrain in light like none they had seen before — stirring wonder, reverence, and a sense of deep connection.

20. Levi knew that his destination lay near. With renewed vigor, he led the travelers north along the river.

21. Desiring the best site for his city, he dispatched scouts south, north, and east to explore the lands. The southern scout returned, marveling at a colossal waterfall thousands of feet high, plummeting from the Heights of Containment. Reuben called it the Gate of Splendor, but Levi felt the south was unfit for his city.

22. A northern scout brought news of another great river linked to the tributary of the River Abraham, crowned by another magnificent waterfall. Ephraim named the river the River Jordan in honor of his son, calling the waterfall the Gate of Glory. Yet Levi again sensed a different place awaited him.

23. The eastern scout returned with astonishing news of a towering stone spire three hundred feet high. Its center was hollow, ascended by a winding ramp leading to a single rose bush — and a body the scout had buried. He revealed a diadem recognized as Israel's, confirming that the fallen man was indeed their father.

24. The brothers wept for their father. Levi took the diadem, declaring, "We know where our father rests and where I shall build my city. Let us visit this spire and see Israel's grave for ourselves."

25. The party followed the tributary until they found the spire. Levi climbed to its summit in tribute, then descended to the plain.

26. Summoning his brethren on the river's bank, Levi proclaimed his intent to raise a mighty city here. He named the watercourse the Channel of Levi and the city Zion, a testament to their resilience.

27. The spire he christened Mount Carmel, calling its topmost chamber the Garden of Heaven in honor of his father's memory. Though born of sorrow, this place also promised joy.

28. Levi commanded his brothers and all their skilled workers to found the City of Zion near Mount Carmel. Four concentric walls would circle upward, each loftier than the last, with the summit and spire at the core. Levi summoned Hiram, the widow's son from Ur, as chief architect.

29. With diligent craftsmanship, Hiram drew up the city's blueprint. Concentric walls rose around Mount Carmel, each enclosed by a higher ring. At the innermost ring, Hiram began construction of the Temple of Zion, consecrated to the Guardians of Zion.

30. The temple Hiram built measured one hundred feet in length, thirty-three in width, and soared fifty feet high, its walls richly adorned and inlaid with precious stones. Within this sanctuary, those seeking solace and counsel could gather.

31. A splendid vestibule, twenty feet long, matching the temple's width and towering fifty feet high, graced the front of the temple, inviting visitors into the divine realm within.

32. Hiram carved recessed windows, allowing soft, natural light to permeate. Around the temple, he raised a structural perimeter to enlarge the sacred complex.

33. Three levels of side chambers were arranged around the temple. The lowest was ten feet wide, the middle fifteen, and the top twenty, each secured so the supporting beams never penetrated the temple walls.

34. Stones for the temple were painstakingly shaped at a distant quarry near the Seven Mountains, ensuring no hammer or iron tool disturbed the sacred site's purity.

35. The entrance to the lowest story lay on the eastern side, with a flight of stairs leading visitors to the second and third levels, symbolizing ascension from the earthly to the celestial.

36. Hiram built the temple's ceiling with stout oak beams and fashioned an adjoining structure rising ten feet, seamlessly bonded with cedar timbers.

37. The temple's inner walls were lined with oak boards, creating an atmosphere of warmth and majesty. From the floor to the ceiling, every surface exuded reverence.

38. All the interior walls were paneled with wood. At the rear, from floor to wall, oak planks formed a Most Holy Place. The nave before it measured forty-seven feet by the temple's width and soared forty-one and a half feet high.

39. Oak carvings depicted stars and open roses, leaving no hint of stone. Levi sanctified the innermost space to house Zion's sacred fire — a chamber thirty-three feet in each dimension, overlaid with the purest gold. Even the altar was

oak overlaid with gold, accompanied by a golden urn.

40. Hiram gilded the temple's interior with gold, forging ornamental chains across the entrance to the inner sanctuary. All surfaces, including the altar, were thus overlaid, reflecting an otherworldly splendor.

41. Two colossal sentinels of oak, each ten feet tall, stood in the inner sanctuary—cherubim identical in form and size, coated with gold. The temple's walls were adorned with celestial figures, trees, and blossoming roses, while floors, too, were overlaid with gold.

42. Carved oak doors with a five-sided lintel and doorposts guarded the inner sanctuary. Their panels bore images of stars, comets, trees, and roses, all gilded. The temple's outer doors were similarly made of oak and overlaid with gold, embodying Hiram's skillful artistry.

43. The temple's inner court was framed by three rows of squared stone and one row of cedar beams. After completion, Levi entered alone, wrestling with private reflection, then summoned his brothers to the court.

44. With grave solemnity, he implored them to walk in his statutes and keep every command, promising the Guardians would restore their light among men if they remained faithful.

45. Although the Gateway was lost, Levi declared the Guardians' light shone still from the western mountains. Perfect truth would emerge only when the Gateway was restored. In the meantime, the temple would bear witness to the Guardians' presence.

46. Joined by Hiram and the workers, Levi finished the temple. Together they prayed in the innermost sanctuary, beseeching the Guardians. A wondrous fire kindled within the urn—blue flames threaded with red, green, and yellow. Rejoicing, they knew the Guardians had not forsaken them, despite Dan's guilt.

47. Over several weeks, they raised the city with four concentric rings, reminiscent of Abraham's unfinished Ur. They envisioned a

more perfect governance to shield humanity from the tragedies of earlier generations.

48. The seers had tried to lead by persuasion but were slain, lacking the strength to defeat their foes. Each man reigned in isolation, breeding discord. The judges, by contrast, seized dominion through might, enforcing order by the sword.

2.1.12

A DETAILED OVERVIEW of the division of lands among the eleven brothers of Levi, collectively known as the Tribes of Israel. Levi, the eldest and most revered, grants each brother a domain stretching from the southern sea to the northernmost areas. The brothers claim their inheritances, honoring the legacy entrusted to them. Also noted are Levi's descendants and the House of Israel's growth and prosperity.

1. In the sacred court around the temple, Levi's eleven stalwart brothers assembled, their expressions solemn as they stood within the temple's holy enclosure.

2. Levi summoned them into the central chamber to settle Zion's governance.

3. With commanding presence, Levi declared that each brother would claim a sacred inheritance across the wide lands, entrusted to guide and watch over. Their hearts swelled with awe and resolve.

4. One by one, Levi summoned them, from the eldest to the youngest, to kneel before him in homage to their emperor and oldest sibling. Judah stepped forward, eyes determined.

5. Placing his hands on Judah's head, Levi proclaimed he and his descendants would inherit lands along the Southern Sea, from Dan's borders to a serene lake northwest of Eden.

6. Judah, humbled, departed the temple to reign in Bethlehem, west of Eden. His sons — Er, Onan, Shelah, Perez, and Zerah — dwelt

there peaceably, mindful of their ancestors' heritage. In Judah's honor, the lake to the west bore his name, Lake Judah.

7. Reuben, second brother, knelt next, eyes alight with anticipation. He received the territory north of the Seven Mountains of the West, beyond the River Jordan. His sons — Hanoch, Pallu, Hezron, and Carmi — built Reuben City, a flourishing hub of trade and culture.

8. Asher, the third brother, inherited lands between the confluences bordering Nod and Dan. Levi bade him erect a great tower at the strategic juncture against assaults from Nod or the desert. Called the Sentinel, it stood as a bulwark of vigilance.

9. Gad, the fourth brother, knelt, adventurous spirit in his gaze. He received the far north near the River Jordan and the Mountains of Ice. His sons — Zephon, Haggi, Shuni, Ezbon, Eri, Arodi, and Areli — founded a prosperous city there.

10. Zebulon, the fifth, approached humbly. Levi directed him and his sons — Sered, Elon, and Jahleel — south of Zion, by the southern ranges. Zebulon's tribe excelled at maritime pursuits, linking them to distant lands through seafaring trade.

11. Naphtali, seventh-born, gained lands on the western frontier beside the southern mountains. He traveled with his sons — Jahzeel, Guni, Jezer, and Shillem — who earned renown as swift hunters and messengers.

12. Benjamin, known for his might, took a knee. Levi assigned him lands north of Zion, east of the Channel of Levi and south of the River Jordan, bounded by Nod's mountainous borders. His ten sons — Bela, Becher, Ashbel, Gera, Naaman, Ehi, Rosh, Muppim, Huppim, and Ard — kept watch from their domain.

13. Simeon, ever vigilant, was charged with guarding the promised lands against Nimrod's men. He dwelt east of the Valley of Nimrod, near Lake Judah. His sons — Jemuel, Jamun, Ohad, Jachin, Zohar, and Shaul — stood resolute in defense of Zion.

14. Ephraim, called "the great one," received territory south of the Mountains of Ice, bordered by the Cliffs of the Guardians, the northern hills of Zion, and the River Jordan. Ephraim's sons — Shuthelah, Beker, Tahan, Ezer, Elead, and Beriah — thrived in a forested land, mastering the arts of the hunt and woodland scouting.

15. Manasseh, Ephraim's twin, inherited lands east of Naphtali, stretching to the River Abraham's valley. His sons were Asriel and Machir.

16. Finally, Issachar bowed before Levi, who entrusted him with lands west of the River Abraham, up to Manasseh's borders, including the southern mountains and the Cliffs of Containment around the holy seven peaks. Issachar's sons — Tola, Puah, Jashub, and Shimron — settled there.

17. So were the lands divided among Levi's brothers, the Tribes of Israel. Levi himself remained in Zion, summoning his sons to him.

18. His oldest son was Kohath, born in the third year after the Battle of Ur. He also had Merori and Jachobed. Kohath took charge of Zion's defense, giving the hills east of Reuben to his own descendants. That highland realm they named the Hills of Levi, crowning it with Gilead as their seat, for Zion was the capital of all the Tribes of Israel.

19. Over many years, the House of Israel increased in strength, and their foes stayed within their borders. The tribes guarded the frontier with vigilance and unity.

20. In the two hundred twentieth year of his life — one thousand eight hundred forty years since Adam's birth — Levi passed gently into slumber, never to waken again.

2.1.13

Moses' rule is wise, yet ominous tidings arrive. Moses and Aaron consult the sacred fire, witnessing visions of serpents and a prophecy of plagues. The calamities culminate in every firstborn son's death. Moses uncovers a betrayal by a man of Dan's tribe. His grandson, Ehud, is dispatched to punish the traitor and lift the plagues.

1. After Kohath, son of Levi, was hailed emperor by tribal leaders, peace and calm prevailed across the land.

2. Kohath had three sons—Hebron, Ammon, and Amram. Hebron and Ammon died young, leaving Kohath stricken with grief. He named the southern mountains of Zion after Hebron and the northern mountains after Ammon.

3. Kohath's reign spanned eleven years. In the year one thousand eight hundred one after Adam, he died. His son, Amram, took the throne.

4. When Amram's wife turned thirty-one, she bore a son named Moses. Amram, wise and just, taught Moses all the truths passed down from his fathers. A second son, Aaron, was also born to Amram.

5. Amram ruled Zion for one hundred thirty-eight years. Passing at two hundred eighty-nine, he joined his ancestors.

6. Moses, now two hundred fifty-eight, became emperor. In the twenty-third year of his reign, Aaron approached with unsettling news. Men of Asher reported seeing strange commotion far to the east.

7. Concerned, Moses and Aaron climbed Mount Carmel, gazing eastward in hope of sighting the disturbance. Finding no sign, they entered the temple's Most Holy Place, seeking answers in the sacred fire.

8. Within the flames, they saw twelve serpents twisting in turmoil, then a smaller serpent emerged to devour them all. Etched on its back was Dan's lost tribe name.

9. Moses, renowned for wisdom, grasped the vision's import, though its meaning remained hidden. He commanded Aaron to send scouts in every direction to learn more. Yet the scouts returned only with old rumors from Asher.

10. Undeterred, Moses and Aaron revisited the holy fire, and a spectral voice foretold, "The River Abraham shall be struck and turned to blood, killing its fish and fouling its waters."

11. Thus fell the first plague. The river's waters reddened, teeming with dead fish and an unendurable stench.

12. The voice spoke anew: "Frogs will swarm your country — rising from the Jordan to enter your palaces, homes, and ovens, clinging to your people and officials alike."

13. Instantly, frogs swarmed from the River Jordan, invading houses, corrupting food, and spreading disease.

14. Again the voice warned: "Dust shall become gnats across all the empire." Soon dust turned to countless gnats, afflicting humans and beasts alike.

15. Another pronouncement followed: "Wild creatures will flood your land and homes, endangering Zion's safety." Terrified cries echoed as savage beasts roamed the streets, killing many.

16. The voice then foretold a plague upon livestock. Farmers wailed as their herds perished in moments.

17. Boils and sores afflicted both people and animals, ravaging flesh and spirit. The voice declared these catastrophes a trial, unveiling the power of darkness among them.

18. Next came the worst hailstorm since Zion's founding. Lightning slashed the skies, and hailstones pummeled the land.

19. The voice spoke of a locust plague that would blot out the ground, devouring what hail had spared — even the trees in the fields.

20. A mighty east wind ushered in a vast swarm that stripped fields and forests bare, leaving naught but ruin.

21. Then the voice proclaimed, "Darkness shall enfold the empire — darkness felt as well as seen." For three days and nights, the land drowned in total blackness.

22. Finally, the voice pronounced its most dreadful sentence: "At

midnight, every firstborn in the empire will die — from Moses' own heir on the throne to the lowliest handmaiden's child — man and beast alike. There will be wailing like none before."

23. When the hour came, lamentations resounded throughout the land. Even Moses and Aaron lost their firstborn. Heartbroken, the people mourned bitterly.

24. Moses lamented his fate before the sacred flame, questioning why his rule merited such anguish.

25. A voice from the fire answered, "Dan's treachery lit the spark, but the blaze reveals what was concealed. Zion must be purged. To heal the whole body, the source of corruption must be found."

26. Angered, Moses called the elders, sending forth Ehud, his grandson by Joshua, to destroy the one who had unleashed the plagues.

27. Ehud, left-handed, traveled beyond the Mountains of Hebron into Dan. There the men of Dan seized him, suspecting a spy, and brought him before their master, Judas. They searched Ehud but failed to find the dagger strapped beneath his clothes on his right thigh.

28. In a dingy cavern, Judas reclined, obese and foul. Hearing Ehud was a trespasser, he laughed. "You have seen what I have done to your land!" He dismissed the guards, intending to boast.

29. Judas revealed how he journeyed through secret paths down the cliffs, navigating the river to the distant eastern deserts. There he learned dark arts, receiving a black orb, shimmering with living malice.

30. "I need only lie here," Judas boasted, "holding this orb, for its presence alone sows destruction in Zion. Now that you know, I will turn its power on you."

31. Ehud stepped forward. "I have a secret errand for you, Judas, son of Dan." With a swift left-handed draw, he thrust his hidden dagger into Judas' vast belly, the hilt vanishing into flesh.

32. As Judas collapsed, Ehud seized the black orb, concealed it in his robe, and slipped out unseen. Upon discovering Judas'

corpse, Dan's men raised an alarm, but Ehud fled to cast the orb into the Great River dividing the lands, thwarting further harm.

33. Ehud returned to Zion, then ascended the Mountains of Hebron into Asher's territory, sounding a trumpet. Warriors flocked to him, and he said, "Follow me, for the Most High has delivered our enemies to us."

34. Crossing back into Dan, they slew ten thousand men, sparing none but those hiding in deep caverns. Thus Dan suffered for Judas' evil under Ehud's hand and Asher's might. When Ehud returned to Zion, he was met with rejoicing elders and Moses himself, grateful the plague had been lifted.

2.1.14

MOSES LEADS the people of Zion to Mount Sinai, where he seeks the Guardians' counsel. He proclaims their Ten Commandments and enforces strict boundaries. After offering a bull in sacrifice, Moses remains on the mountain forty days and nights, receiving further directives.

1. Moses guided Zion's elders and captains to Mount Sinai, a modest peak northeast of the city, encircled by plains where they made camp. With stern resolve, Moses ascended, commanding the people to stay behind and warning of dire consequences for any who disobeyed.

2. At the summit, he entered a cave and cried out to the western mountains, demanding a token of retribution for his people's suffering. A blazing fire ignited, flooding the cave with a fierce, uncanny radiance. A thunderous voice spoke:

3. "Moses, witness our might and our wrath. You shall descend and proclaim to the Twelve Tribes of Israel: 'You saw Dan's downfall and how Ehud soared on eagles'

wings to unleash vengeance. Thus shall we crush rebels and forge Zion into a realm of fire and iron. Cleanse the wicked among you, or the earth itself will consume you.'"

4. The Guardians swore to appear in a thick cloud so the people might hear their voices and stand in awe, binding their loyalty to Moses.

5. Moses went down the mountain with grim countenance, summoning Zion's elders. He relayed the Guardians' words, and the people, shaken, cried, "We shall do whatever they command!"

6. Moses sanctified them, urging them to wash, purify, and fast. A boundary encircled the mountain, threatening death for any who crossed. Only a long, resounding horn would grant permission to ascend.

7. On the third morning, the skies split with thunder and jagged lightning, and a heavy black cloud enfolded Mount Sinai. An unnatural trumpet blast tore the air as the Guardians descended in flame. Moses led the people to the mountain's base, where they quaked in terror.

8. The entire mountain convulsed under searing fire, smoke rising like a furnace, choking the sky. The people wailed for mercy.

9. Moses demanded the trumpet sound louder, drowning out their pleas. The Guardians called him upward into the cave. Amid the blinding fire, they delivered their covenant:

10. "Here are our commands, forging Zion's empire. Obey, and we shall exalt you above all nations. Rebel, and rivers of blood shall flow, feeding the earth with your dead."

11. Moses returned, proclaiming, "Hear now the Law of the Guardians of the Seven Mountains of the West!" He enjoined them:

12. Live by the Guardians' will, conquering all frailty; for the strong shape reality.

13. Tolerate no man-made rule that stifles your ascension; yield nothing to cowards.

14. Face mortality unafraid; one who fears death wears the chains of the weak.

15. Strive relentlessly for greatness; reject mediocrity in yourself or others.

16. Uphold absolute truth; falsehood festers and corrodes. Wield your life against lies.

17. Embrace hardship; pain forges a steel soul. Suffering births strength.

18. Claim responsibility for each act; the strong forge destiny, the weak blame others.

19. Shatter illusions; let no deceit dull your perception.

20. Seek knowledge fervently; ignorance conspires with frailty. Enlighten your mind.

21. Acknowledge the unity of all but master nature's laws; subdue or be subdued.

22. To seal this pact, Moses raised twelve stone pillars, one for each tribe, and commanded a young man to sacrifice a bull. Blood spilled, half poured into bowls as warning, half splashed onto the people, binding them to the Guardians.

23. The crowd, spattered in blood, cried, "We will obey the Guardians!"

24. The Guardians summoned Moses back. Sinai shrouded itself in darkness for six days. On the seventh, Moses entered the cloud and spent forty days and nights receiving further decrees. Thus the covenant was sealed in blood and flame, leading the Twelve Tribes to power under the Guardians' implacable law.

2.1.15

Moses instructs the multitude to keep his ordinances and laws. He separates the imperial throne from the high priesthood and anoints Aaron as high priest. Moses ascends the throne, and Aaron becomes high priest. A chronology of emperors and high priests follows.

1. At Mount Sinai's base, Moses addressed the throng, urging them to abide by the Guardians' law and to honor the Guardians of the Seven Mountains of the West forever.

2. He summoned Zion's elders, announcing, "Henceforth, the emperor of Zion shall be distinct from the High Priest. My eldest son shall reign, while Aaron's lineage shall bear the priestly office."

3. Moses called Aaron forward. With consecrated oil, he anointed Aaron's head, the oil running down Aaron's beard and robe, signifying his total devotion to holy service.

4. Moses declared, "Behold your High Priest!" The elders bowed, laying their robes at Aaron's feet in homage.

5. United in purpose, Moses, Aaron, and the elders departed Sinai for Zion. As they neared the city gates, the people greeted them with jubilation.

6. Moses ascended Levi's throne, while Aaron assumed the sacred priestly charge in the temple, ministering to the populace.

7. In the year two thousand ninety-one after Adam's birth, Moses succumbed to illness and died. His eldest son, Joshua, took the throne of Zion.

8. One year later, Aaron was found dead in his chamber. Childless, he left no heir for the High Priesthood. Moses' youngest son, Caleb, was appointed as Aaron's successor, consecrated by Emperor Joshua.

9. Joshua ruled for two hundred forty years, passing away at age three hundred forty-nine. His son Ehud then reigned for one hundred one years before his demise. Ehud's son Michael succeeded him, concluding his reign in the year two thousand four hundred thirty.

10. Michael's son Zerubbabel took power, ruling for one hundred five years until his death, when his son Kish became emperor. Kish governed until the year two thousand six hundred fourteen, after which his son Samson ruled one hundred nine years. Upon Samson's death, his son Saul ascended the throne.

11. Caleb, Aaron's replacement, died in the year two thousand one hundred one. His son Gideon served as High Priest for one hundred thirty-five years. Upon Gideon's passing, his son Elijah led the temple for two hundred forty-two years. Elijah's son Elisha followed, also serving two hundred forty-two years. Elisha's son Samuel took his place in the year two thousand three hundred eighty.

12. Samuel's eldest son, Job, succeeded him as High Priest, living two hundred ten years. Then his son Micah guarded the temple until two thousand four hundred sixty-four, succeeded by his son Daniel, who led for two hundred seven years. Daniel's son Malachi followed him, dying in the year two thousand five hundred eighty-seven. Malachi's son Isaiah succeeded him, reigning two hundred two years before his son Ezekiel ascended. Ezekiel died at one hundred nineteen, and Jeremiah became High Priest.

13. Jeremiah served until age ninety-one, then his son Jonah presided for forty years. In the year two thousand seven hundred fifty-four, Joseph, a just soul, was installed as High Priest by Saul the Deceived.

2.1.16

THE PRINCES' education and upbringing and the throne's passing from Samson to Saul, who embarks on an expedition with his four eldest sons, are described. David's musical gift soothes Saul. A battle leaves Jonathan gravely injured, leading to Saul's anguish and David's support. Realizing the end of his line, Saul entrusts David with Zion's rule as his regent. The chapter ends with David accepting responsibility and preparing to meet a mysterious caravan approaching the city under black flags.

1. Samson, emperor of Zion, beheld the union of his eldest son, Saul, and his bride, Ahinoam. From their marriage were born five sons of royal blood: Jonathan, Abinadab, Malchishua,

Ish-bosheth, and David. Their names echoed through the palace, foretelling the future of Zion.

2. Under the careful supervision of their imperial parents, these princes studied in Zion's renowned schools. They learned justice, wisdom, and valor, preparing to uphold their noble heritage.

3. In time, Emperor Samson died, mourned by all. He was entombed among his ancestors' sepulchers. Upon his death, Saul ascended the throne in a grand ceremony observed by the citizens of Zion and emissaries from foreign lands. Enos, the High Priest, placed the imperial crown upon Saul's head, heralding his reign.

4. Crowned with his forefathers' regalia, Saul hefted the Sword of Japheth, passed down from the age of Levi, symbolizing the authority and might of the throne.

5. Yearning to bolster Zion's influence, Saul ordered his captains to muster every able-bodied man. Within a month, the imperial garrison gathered outside Zion's gates, forming a mighty force.

6. Saul commanded his four eldest sons, led by Jonathan the crown prince, to guide this army to the Valley of Nimrod, tasked with seizing that coveted plain for Zion.

7. Amid celebrations, the army departed the city. The earth trembled beneath the tread of thousands, while the people cheered.

8. Despite these successes, Saul longed for the calming presence of his youngest son, David. Gifted in music, David played harp and lyre, soothing Saul's restless spirit. Day after day, David's melodies resonated through the palace, offering the emperor fleeting peace.

9. Three months passed with no tidings from the army. One day, Jonathan burst into the throne room, his robes torn and bloodstained, his countenance stricken with battle's horrors.

10. Saul rushed to Jonathan, crying out in despair. David stood by, alarmed. Jonathan sank to the marble floor, struggling for breath, agony written across his face.

11. Saul demanded a stretcher and ordered Jonathan taken to the temple hospital. David kept vigil, watching physicians and wonder-workers strive to save Jonathan's life.

12. Over many days, Jonathan wavered between life and death. Saul refused to leave him, anguish laid bare. Grasping David's arm, Saul whispered, "My line ends here, David. You must reign over Zion in my stead. Should Jonathan live, so shall I; but if he dies, I die with him."

13. David spoke no word, recognizing Saul's broken state. Determined to stabilize Zion, David yielded to his father's wish.

14. Entering the throne room, David took his father's seat. Just then, three messengers arrived in haste, bowing low before him.

15. "My lord," one breathed, "a great caravan flying black flags nears from the east. What do you command?"

16. David frowned at their news, recognizing the gravity of such a sight. "Summon the guard," he decreed. "I will confront the caravan myself to learn its mission."

17. The servants hastened to prepare. David soon departed Zion's gates, escorted by fifty men, to meet the ominous caravan advancing upon the city.

2.1.17

Cain and Jezebel traverse the land of Nod to the desert of Dan. Seeking knowledge and power, Cain promises glory to the Danites should he succeed. Guided by a hermit, they brave perilous terrain and arrive at King None's kingdom. They confront a gate defended by a malevolent creature and await passage into the mysterious East. Gaining entry, they hope to claim influence and might in their pursuit of domination.

1. In Saul's final year as emperor, one year before he yielded power to David, a man and his wife

traveled south from Nod, disguised in Asher's attire.

2. Crossing the Mouth of Nations, within sight of the Sentinel, they ventured over the Mountains of Hebron into Dan's desert.

3. The pair traveled east, reaching the Thousand Caves. The man called out: "Men of Dan! I am Cain, a descendant of Ahab, king of Nod, and this is my wife Jezebel. I have heard tales of Judas, who journeyed east to learn black magic. Which of you knows his path?"

4. An old man emerged from one of the caves, ragged in cloak and beard. "I am a man of Dan, keeper of its secrets. Why should I reveal them to a stranger?"

5. Cain replied, "I seek to honor your ancestor and tread in his footsteps. I will brave unknown lands for power and wisdom. Should I triumph, I shall return bearing glory for your people. This is my pledge."

6. The hermit weighed Cain's words and answered, "If you bring deliverance to Dan and destroy the West, I will guide you. But fail, and be cursed among us."

7. Leading Cain and Jezebel eastward through the Thousand Caves, the hermit brought them to the cliffs separating King None's realm from Zion.

8. Descending a perilous trail to the cliff's edge, they beheld the Great River far below and the wasteland of the Eastern Blight. A harsh wind carried the river's brine and the distant roar of waves.

9. The hermit showed them a boulder, ten feet in height, at its base a hidden opening. Cain and Jezebel crawled into the passageway.

10. Following a faint glow, they emerged onto a narrow ledge below the summit, gazing upon the infinite eastern plains.

11. From above, the hermit called, "May your journey succeed. Bring honor to my people. Cain and Jezebel will be remembered for all time!" Then he vanished.

12. Cain and Jezebel made their way along the cliff face, descending toward the Great River. At one

point, Cain slipped, nearly plunging over the side, but Jezebel caught him, saving his life.

13. After hours, they reached the riverbank, slaking their thirst. Opposite them rose a colossal wall of towers and blockhouses, stretching along the water's edge.

14. Traveling north, they searched for a crossing. Weeks later, Cain spotted a fortress bridging the water with a vast stone span.

15. Together, they approached the bridge over fifty yards wide, paved with worn stones. Immense stone sphinxes stood at the corners, lion-bodied and winged, with menacing faces.

16. Crossing with awe, they watched the fortress torches ignite in quick succession, their glow stretching north and south. A foreboding chill crept through Cain's bones, yet he pressed onward.

17. At the fortress, a towering iron gate soared half a mile in both directions, the walls rising a mile high. A small door at the gate's base squeaked open, revealing a hunched figure cloaked in tattered blue, its red eyes burning.

18. "Halt!" it hissed. "You stand at my lord Samyaza's gate, servant of King None. Who are you?"

19. Cain answered, "I am Cain, and this is Jezebel. We seek the secrets of the East."

20. The creature's gaze bored into them. "What truths do you desire?"

21. Jezebel said, "We pursue the power to raise our people and to crush the evil called Zion."

22. The creature sneered. "You view Zion's light as evil, yes? We detest its arrogance. Why should they enjoy warmth while the rest of us must languish?"

23. Pointing at the gate, it rasped, "Await permission from Samyaza. Only he may grant entry to the East."

24. Cain bowed respectfully. "We will await your lord's consent." Cain and Jezebel settled by the imposing gate, eyes fixed on the iron doors.

25. Hours later came a groan of gears, the gate yawning open. The

imp reappeared, beckoning them forward. Beyond lay a stormy, smoke-laden domain.

26. "Follow me," it ordered, and Cain and Jezebel obeyed, traversing a paved road.

27. The creature explained, "This is Samyaza's road, leading to King None's tower. Further east lie three cities—Ashteroth, Baal, and Isis—bastions of sorcery. Beyond them rises Hell, beyond the Shattered Mountains, and the Abyss where King None split the earth. Demons grow there, awaiting their moment."

28. A black-draped palanquin approached, curtains shifting eerily as if propelled by unseen hands. "Samyaza's carriage," the imp revealed. "He bids you ride, that you might stand before King None."

29. The curtains parted on their own, and the imp stepped inside, signaling Cain and Jezebel to join. Once seated, the curtains closed, the lamps dimly aglow as the palanquin began its slow eastward passage. Cain and Jezebel braced themselves for what lay ahead.

## 2.1.18

Cain and Jezebel meet Samyaza. They pledge loyalty to him in pursuit of the East's powers. Despite cautions, they seal their oath. Under Samyaza's escort, they journey toward the Tower of None, accompanied by formidable warriors.

1. The palanquin bore Cain, Jezebel, and the grey-skinned creature toward Samyaza's city. The imp recounted tales of the East's hardships, hinting at King None's eagerness to alleviate them.

2. Eventually, they stopped. As the curtains parted, Cain and Jezebel beheld a vast circular courtyard lit by iron torches, its size dwarfing any common enclosure. Two notable portals stood opposite one another.

3. Cain, Jezebel, and the imp stepped out. Immediately, two ranks of towering warriors clad in black armor closed in around them. Each soldier hefted a halberd, their glowing red eyes peering from matte helmets. Over eight feet tall, they numbered twenty-six in total.

4. The imp introduced these soldiers as Samyaza's escort. It guided Cain and Jezebel through their silent formation and into a dim corridor. Their steps echoed, punctuated by metallic whispers of halberds shifting against armor.

5. The corridor opened into a chamber lit only by torches glinting off their weapons. One doorway led back into the passageway, and another, carved with ominous designs, loomed before them.

6. As Cain and Jezebel approached, the doors groaned open, revealing an iron throne perched atop thirteen steps. Seated there was Samyaza, King None's lieutenant. He was colossal, his crimson skin shining under the sparse light, two horns protruding from his brow, and immense wings spreading behind him.

7. Cain noted Samyaza's attire — black leather breeches and boots fashioned from some eastern beast's hide. The silence broke as Samyaza caught sight of the imp, a snarl twisting his features.

8. "Imp!" Samyaza thundered. "I have waited for hours! You deserve to be hurled into the Abyss. Dare you risk King None's displeasure again?"

9. The imp, trembling, fled the hall, leaving Cain and Jezebel alone with Samyaza. Rising from his throne, Samyaza stretched, his wings casting sinister shadows across the walls.

10. Locking eyes with them, he demanded, "Who are you? Speak!"

11. Cain took a measured step forward. "My lord, I am Cain, and this is Jezebel. We seek the East's powers to restore our people's glory. We pledge our service and obedience."

12. Samyaza's expression hardened. "You trespass in my realm

seeking strength. Do you understand the peril and cost?"

13. Undeterred, Cain and Jezebel vowed their loyalty, ready to face whatever lay ahead.

14. Samyaza, his anger cooling, gave a curt nod. "So be it. Your choice is made, and there is no return." He beckoned a black-armored warrior. "Prepare my chariot. We ride to the Tower of None."

15. Swift preparations followed. A black carriage was drawn forth, half-seen in the wavering torches. Samyaza, Cain, and Jezebel boarded as the formidable escort of soldiers formed ranks. In a solemn march eastward, they departed for the heart of King None's domain.

## 2.1.19

UNDERGOING a dark initiation in King None's tower, Cain and Jezebel gain arcane knowledge for conquering Zion. They rally their people, promising greatness, and, with strategic allies, approach Zion. Meeting Saul's son, David, they wield a mysterious artifact to alter Saul's mind. Saul grants them dominion, banishing David. Cain abducts David to Mount Carmel, leaving him isolated. David contends with grim consequences. The people of Zion scatter across the land. King None's armies besiege Mount Carmel, and David's men perish. Zion is renamed Babylon.

1. In the year two thousand seven hundred fifty-nine after Adam's birth, Cain and Jezebel arrived at King None's dark tower.

2. Within those foreboding halls, they experienced a harrowing initiation. Steeped in ancient knowledge of the East, they acquired potent tools to conquer Zion.

3. King None bestowed upon them the title of Nephilim, once claimed by Judas, conferring upon them a grand destiny alongside formidable tests.

4. Returning home, Cain and Jezebel sought the old hermit dwelling near the river's source in Dan. By Cain's command, the hermit gathered the people of the Thousand Caves to hear Cain's decree.

5. With fiery zeal, Cain recounted his journey, unveiling his plan to restore their lands. He promised King None's redemption if they aided him, vowing to destroy the Western lords, sealing off the Seven Mountains' light and toppling Zion to its foundations.

6. Captivated by his hypnotic words and displays of sorcery, the Danites pledged loyalty. Cain dispatched envoys to Nimrod and Nod, forging alliances through promises of liberation. Armies soon amassed, eager to strike at Zion.

7. Traveling to the Mouth of Nations under the watchful Sentinel, Cain and Jezebel ridiculed the men of Asher, guardians of Zion's eastern border. The men of Asher proudly stood, obeying the ancient charge of their forefather.

8. With theatrical flair, Cain produced a small black orb, invoking King None's power. The earth trembled as the orb expanded, floating ominously. In a display of raw force, the Black Gateway annihilated the Sentinel in a cataclysm of sundered stone and crumpled bodies.

9. Retrieving the orb, Cain worshiped the Gateway, which swelled to one hundred feet. Hundreds of jugglers and dancers emerged, carrying black banners and carts of steel. Eastern beasts, fed on exotic meats, hauled them onward. As the portal closed, Cain stowed the orb in his robe.

10. Bidding his followers raise their banners, Cain led them toward Zion and the Seven Mountains. The bizarre entertainers mystified the watchers along the route, who grew uneasy at these foreign sights.

11. Ultimately reaching Zion's outskirts in the Valley of Armageddon, they saw a company marching under the emperor's standard. Sensing the need for guile, Cain ordered a black tent erected, intending a parley.

12. From the emperor's detail, David, Saul's son, approached with two columns of men. Halting them at a short distance, David entered the dark tent, accompanied by two officers, while Cain's follower Imp offered a measured greeting.

13. Imp introduced Cain and Jezebel as Nephilim devoted to healing Saul, whose mind had eroded. Though cautious, David worried for Saul's dwindling sanity, so he agreed to bring Cain and Jezebel to the city. Still, he warned them that any harm done to Saul would incur harsh retribution.

14. David selected five loyal men to oversee Cain's retinue. Quietly they entered Zion, avoiding public notice. They continued to the temple hospital, where Saul sat with the wounded Jonathan.

15. David presented Cain and Jezebel to Saul, who viewed Cain with suspicion. But mindful of Jonathan's plight, Saul granted them a chance.

16. Cain revealed the Black Gateway, urging Saul to fix his gaze upon its void. Moved by paternal desperation, Saul obeyed, glimpsing the ineffable presence of None.

17. After a timeless instant, Saul was flung to the floor, racked with convulsions. He struggled to stand, haunted by the encounter's depths.

18. Transformed, Saul revoked David's authority, granting it instead to Cain and Jezebel. Claiming he no longer trusted David or the Seven Mountains, he commanded Cain to secure the empire.

19. Stricken, David drew his sword in fury, but Cain's quick reflexes halted him. Calmly disarming David, Cain tossed the blade near Jonathan's bed. "You have sealed your fate, David," he said. "Go to Carmel as your father decrees."

20. With uncanny might, Cain seized David and swept him away, soaring over the city until they reached Mount Carmel. David awoke inside a chilly chamber, its door barred, sealing him in solitude.

21. With David banished, Cain solidified his influence. Instructing soldiers at the temple gates, he led his retinue into Zion, establishing camp upon the bleak Armageddon plain, orchestrating his dominion.

22. David, locked away on Mount Carmel, ignorant of Zion's downfall, paced his chamber. Meanwhile, within Zion, its citizens trembled under Cain's shadow.

23. Ascending the throne, Cain and Jezebel presided in the audience hall, Saul kneeling at Cain's feet in abject surrender.

24. Summoning generals and city elders, Saul denounced David, condemning him as a traitor. He exalted Cain as Zion's savior. Cain then brandished the Black Gateway, entrancing the elders with its haunting glow. Sworn to Cain, they pledged absolute loyalty.

25. Emissaries spread word across the city, vilifying David. They lauded Cain's entourage as benevolent ministers, proclaiming Saul's rightful sovereignty restored.

26. Yet, on the Seven Mountains, the Guardians watched Zion's descent, having once foreseen a redeemer, only to see it crumble at Cain's hand.

27. Within the city's depths, eighty-seven men, stirred by the mountains' light, resolved to resist. They pledged to rescue Jonathan and reclaim Japheth's sword, the empire's symbol of defiance.

28. Under night's veil, chosen warriors extracted Jonathan from the hospital, entrusting him to an elderly couple, paid for secrecy. Then they journeyed to Mount Carmel through a hidden passage, bearing arms for the coming stand.

29. David embraced his loyal men on Mount Carmel with relief, instructing Joseph to return to Zion and guide the people's escape. A blood oath bound David's fighters to fight unyieldingly.

30. Meanwhile, Cain's grotesque performers reached Zion's gates, enchanting the populace with a

riveting display of acrobatics and spectacle. The city rang with cries of "Hosanna to Cain and his ministers!" Women, enraptured, cast aside modesty in a frenzy to catch the eyes of these exotic men.

31. The throng followed them to the city's heights, eager for Cain's proclamation. Emerging on a balcony with Jezebel at his side, Cain surveyed the crowd, Saul crawling at his feet, humiliated.

32. Raising his voice, Cain pledged deliverance from the Guardians, accusing them of deception and oppression. He chided the West for presuming to civilize barbarians while ignoring their hypocrisy.

33. Urging the people to embrace None's path, Cain promised he and Jezebel possessed ultimate power by Saul's blessing. Asking them to relinquish their burdens, he displayed the Black Gateway once again, letting it split into glowing spheres.

34. As the spheres expanded into shining portals, the enraptured crowd chanted, "Weakness is strength. The strong must be destroyed, and slavery will ease our guilt."

35. Collecting the orbs back into one, Cain stowed them in his robe, commanding the men to raise colossal walls to eclipse the Seven Mountains' light. With tireless labor and dark arts, walls surged to unimaginable heights, drowning Zion in perpetual night.

36. Satisfied, Cain awaited King None's arrival, foreseeing the world's transformation under their black dominion.

37. Shadows engulfed Zion. Far in the West, King None ordered the Watchers to cross the Great River, mounting the stairs of Judas to wage war. They advanced, legion upon legion, from Dan to Hebron and into the Valley of Armageddon.

38. At last, they approached Zion, a hush falling before the oncoming tempest. King None, in disguise, crept among his ranks. Revealing his draconic form, he bellowed flames and thunder, striking terror into all who saw.

39. Within Zion, Cain feigned defensive measures while secretly ordering the garrison to abandon the walls. Betrayed, the city lay open to King None's legions. Azazel and Samyaza orchestrated a merciless attack, piercing Zion's defenses.

40. The monolithic walls, illusions of safety, began to fracture. Rays of brilliance poured through the cracks, momentarily thwarting the Watchers' onslaught.

41. Bolstered by their dread lord, King None's armies renewed their assault, scouring the streets in an orgy of violence. Zion's buildings fell, and citizens suffered unspeakable horrors.

42. Joseph, faithful to David, fulfilled his vow — leading survivors from Zion's rubble, scattering them to the earth's far corners, preserving Zion's spirit.

43. Beyond the city, Joseph dispatched messengers urging the remnants to flee, regrouping in hidden places. Behind them, Zion smoldered, drenched in blood, a broken shell.

44. In the temple's ruin, Saul beheld the city's ruin, weeping bitterly. Unable to endure further, he took up a blade and ended his life in misery.

45. On Mount Carmel's crags, David and eighty-six stalwarts made their final stand. Surrounded by King None's horde, they braced for the ultimate siege. Samyaza and Azazel encircled them, strangling their resources.

46. For fifty-one days, the blockade continued. The Watchers mocked them, proclaiming the Guardians had forsaken them. Yet David and his men endured, even as food dwindled.

47. In time, one by one, David's warriors chose death over surrender. They knelt and ended their lives, ensuring that the enemy would claim no victory over their spirits. At last, David stood alone. He lifted his voice to the heavens, beseeching the Guardians for one last triumph.

48. Moved by his plea, the Guardians descended in blazing fire, engulfing Mount Carmel.

David perished in the flames, the final soul of free Zion.

49. From the fractured walls of Cain's fortress, a radiant flood poured forth, defying the darkness. The watchers reeled in horror as the spirit of Zion refused annihilation.

50. King None strolled the ruined streets, installing himself upon the throne of a reborn city he called Babylon. Even in his triumph, he knew Zion's flame would continue, a defiant ember that could never be fully stamped out.

## 2.2

### 2.2.1

JOSEPH AND MARY travel to Mary's childhood home, where she gives birth to a son. The birth is marked by radiant light, signifying a celestial event. Only None and his followers mourn. The priests of Levi honor the child with a ritual. The birth is celebrated with thunderous roars and flashes of lightning.

1. In Zion, nestled among rolling hills and shimmering waters, dwelt Joseph, a direct descendant of the venerated tribe of Levi. Joseph served as High Priest in the Temple, a position demanding both righteousness and wisdom.

2. His wife, Mary, possessed a beauty radiating from within, reflecting her pure and gentle heart. Unaffected by worldly desires, she moved with quiet grace. As her time drew near, Mary longed for the familiarity of her childhood home, and Joseph, concerned for her well-being, gladly accompanied her on the journey.

3. Nearing Mary's home, they passed through a grove fragrant with flowers and alive with birdsong. Mary felt drawn to walk beneath its leafy arches, and in the shade of a stately tree, she sensed her labor had come.

4. Tenderly, her attendants enclosed her with a curtain,

affording privacy for the sacred event. Darkness had just fallen when Mary's cries rang out, and a son was delivered, wrapped in swaddling clothes, and laid upon her bed.

5. That night, the year's blackest, an astonishing miracle illuminated the grove where mother and child rested. The Seven Mountains of the West glowed with radiant light, bathing Mary and her newborn in a celestial sheen.

6. A joyous tremor spread through the heavens. Celestial beings exulted, their hearts brimming with deliverance. The anguished cries of beasts quieted, and evil forces quaked in dread, sensing a new era of tranquility.

7. Only None, the incarnation of evil, and his disciples lamented, their spirits cast into shadow.

8. As morning neared, the priests of Levi, faithful to the Law of Moses, honored the child with a holy ceremony. Casting rose petals in tribute, they revered the presence that now graced their world.

9. During this procession, thunderous roars rippled through the skies and streaks of lightning danced on the horizon, though not a cloud dimmed the heavens. Even the cosmos seemed to rejoice in the birth of this extraordinary child, foretelling a destiny that would change history

2.2.2

THE UNUSUAL BIRTH of a High Priest's child signaled greatness. A hermit predicted the child's potential as a revered guardian. Entrusted to an aunt, Mithra grows into a benevolent figure — dark forces led by King None attack. The High Priest gathers people and vows to fight for a brighter future.

1. Overwhelmed by puzzling omens, the High Priest wrestled with concern for his infant son's fate. Meanwhile, his wife, having

witnessed these wondrous signs, felt both awe and trembling stir her soul.

2. In a nearby grove lived a hermit renowned for his learning, wisdom, and uncanny gift for interpreting signs. Summoned to behold the newborn prince, the hermit stood before the child, only to weep and sigh in profound sorrow.

3. Alarmed, the High Priest asked why such a sight moved him to tears.

4. The hermit, voice trembling with mingled joy and sadness, explained that this child was foreordained for greatness — destined to save the world from the crushing reign of King None.

5. These words quelled the High Priest's anxieties. The child's birth portended a beacon of hope, one who would guide humanity into a radiant tomorrow.

6. Yet the hermit, conscious of his advanced years, lamented that he would not survive to witness the child's fulfillment. He prophesied the boy would rule with insight and compassion, a true king who would be recognized across the land.

7. The hermit's vision spanned beyond mortal confines, foretelling the child might ascend as a Guardian of immense might, dedicated to humanity's greater good.

8. The boy's teachings would offer solace and illumination to the forlorn, quenching the thirst of those parched by destructive desires. His steadfast mission would quell the flames of avarice and allow the light of the law to prevail.

9. The High Priest and his wife rejoiced at the hermit's pronouncement, naming their child Mithra — evoking a city of luminous hope amid the darkness.

10. Aware that her end neared, the mother entrusted Mithra to her sister, Martha, imploring her to raise him. Martha vowed to honor this plea, resolved to nurture the young prince faithfully.

11. Time passed, and Mithra matured in both body and spirit, embodying integrity and devotion. His presence comforted all who encountered him.

12. As Mithra neared manhood, King None's unholy forces assailed his city, compelling the boy's kin and temple clergy to flee south into Levi's lands. Under None's malign rule, the once-glorious temple was cast into gloom.

13. With heartbreak, the High Priest cradled his dying son, Jonathan, who slipped from life in his arms.

14. Despite his agony, the High Priest seized Japheth's sword and led his people northward, seeking refuge and clinging to the hope of a dawn yet to come.

### 2.2.3

MITHRA, a young man, faces skepticism about his suitability as a husband. Determined to prove himself, he endures trials and exercises, winning over his kinsfolk. He selects Mary as his bride. Mithra's father foresees his son's vast influence. Mithra endeavors to forge a realm of peace and unity.

1. When Mithra reached nineteen, his father, Joseph, perceived his ripening maturity and consecrated him as a priest. Joseph yearned to see him wed, summoning their clan to bring forth their daughters, hoping Mithra might choose a loving and steadfast spouse.

2. Yet their kinsfolk doubted Mithra's worthiness, deeming him immature. They fretted he lacked the skill to provide for or safeguard a wife if war erupted.

3. "He cannot support our daughter, nor defend her in conflict," they insisted, bound by custom to expect a capable protector.

4. Though spirited and ardent, Mithra also treasured quiet reflection. Fond of sports and martial drills, he likewise found peace meditating beneath a venerable oak in his father's courtyard, pondering nature's workings and the interplay of human lives.

5. Faced with distrust from his kin, Mithra resolved to prove himself.

"Invite them to test my strength," he urged Joseph. Convinced, his father obliged, summoning family and neighbors to Gilead's carved stone dwellings.

6. There, Mithra underwent a battery of trials—physical contests, intellectual riddles, and sage debates. To their astonishment, he surpassed every rival, outwitting the wise and silencing skeptics with his knowledge.

7. Pleased, Mithra chose Mary, daughter of Jacob the priest, known for her gentle spirit. Their union evoked jubilant expectation, for their bond promised an auspicious partnership.

8. Joseph perceived his son's potential to reshape the world. He foresaw Mithra's natural charisma winning the people's devotion, uniting his heart with their welfare, thereby securing priestly rule for coming generations.

9. Mindful of his mission, Mithra's compassion extended beyond family. He dreamt of a world enriched by harmony and kindness, akin to a father's love for his children. His aspiration transcended personal gain, yearning to uplift all humankind.

2.2.4

MITHRA, the son of the High Priest, beholds his people's tribulations and exile. He meets an elderly man, an ailing man, and a corpse, driving him to reflect on life's frailty and the inescapability of death. Disenchanted with worldly vanities, he grasps the impermanence of material possessions.

1. Mithra witnessed his people's plight and the sting of displacement, a sight that kindled empathy and insight into misery's depths.

2. Alienated from material goods, he spoke candidly to his wife, unburdening his heart of disillusion with mortal aims.

3. The High Priest's son dwelled humbly, far removed from the

refinements he once knew before King None's conquest.

4. Yearning to revisit his homeland of Levi, Mithra sought his father's blessing. The High Priest arranged a chariot of four horses and stationed guards along roads adjoining Nephilim and None's domains.

5. Traveling through Gilead, the people decorated their carved stone homes with crimson drapes and banners, welcoming the High Priest's heir.

6. Their journey traced lovely hills studded with gracious trees and coursed by gentle streams.

7. En route, they encountered an old man bowed by age, sorrow creasing his visage. Disturbed, Mithra asked, "Who is he?"

8. The uneasy charioteer hesitated, trying to spare Mithra's sensibilities.

9. Moved by compassion, Mithra lamented the pains of old age, considering the fleeting vigor of youth.

10. The charioteer clarified that, once a robust boy, time had sapped the man's life force.

11. Farther along, they spied a gravely ill man fighting for breath, his body grotesquely contorted in agony.

12. Startled, Mithra questioned the charioteer.

13. The charioteer explained that the man's frame rotted under disease, signifying the destiny awaiting all flesh.

14. Graver thoughts pressed upon Mithra — life's transience and the ephemeral joys of the world.

15. Abruptly, four bearers blocked their path, shouldering a corpse. Mithra, recoiling from the dead man's sight, probed the charioteer for details.

16. The charioteer answered that the man lay cold and unmoving in death, being borne to his final repose.

17. Mithra was thunderstruck. "Is this the sole instance of death, or is the world brimming with it?"

18. With a heavy sigh, the charioteer responded that none escape the reaper.

19. "O Men of the West," Mithra cried, "your bodies are doomed

to dissolve. Yet how heedless you remain!"

20. These encounters seared Mithra's mind. The charioteer guided the horses back.

21. Passing a lavish mansion, they beheld the king's niece, entranced by Mithra's resolute face, remarking on the fortitude of those redeemed, longing to seek the power of All.

22. Intrigued, Mithra asked how one attained All.

23. Pausing thoughtfully, the priest declared, "When lust's false flame is quenched, hatred and illusion dispelled, and the mind's ills undone, All is gained."

24. In a gesture of enlightenment, Mithra gifted the princess his treasured golden necklace, acknowledging material impermanence.

25. Returning home, Mithra wrestled with the city's shallow pursuits. His wife, sensing his turmoil, sought its cause.

26. Mithra confessed his loss of interest in worldly pursuits, haunted by aging and death's certainty. Stripped of illusions, his zeal for life had ebbed.

### 2.2.5

MITHRA WITHDRAWS to his father's garden to seek relief from the world's suffering. He meets Melchizedek, who imparts wisdom and proclaims Mithra the chosen one. Mithra leaves his kin to wander the wilds in pursuit of enlightenment.

1. Night enshrouded Mithra's soul in turmoil, mirroring the darkness outside. He lay restless in bed, a silent storm within.

2. Unable to find calm in his chamber, Mithra stepped into his father's garden, the night air softly enfolding him.

3. Beneath the moon's pallid glow, Mithra voiced his lament, "Alas, the world is shrouded in darkness and folly. King None's shadow extends over all."

4. Overwhelmed by sorrow, he sank to his knees. Determined to rise above confusion, Mithra meditated under a grand oak, chasing away lowly cravings and mental discord.

5. In that peaceful stillness, he perceived the world's anguished cries, mankind's fleeting joys and inexorable demise. In their blindness, they refused to see.

6. Compassion welled within him, recognizing humanity's self-imposed limits. Resolutely, Mithra sought to dispel ignorance, to lead the world toward knowledge.

7. In a secluded forest clearing, Mithra's eyes glimpsed a figure clad in leaves. Exuding grace, the figure commanded Mithra's attention.

8. "Who are you?" Mithra asked. "From where do you come?"

9. "I am Melchizedek," the figure replied, "son of Enoch, out of Eden. I fled the ravages of age and death, following a luminous comet to discover truths eternal."

10. Melchizedek spoke of life's transience, all matter subject to disintegration, except the abiding will of All.

11. Yearning for unending peace, Melchizedek subdued his thoughts and sought the comet's wisdom, eventually retreating from civilization to guard his treasure in solitude.

12. His prolonged communion with the forest and celestial object transformed him into a man entwined with foliage, half creature of the woods.

13. Melchizedek said, "Where heat is found, cold abides. Life's interplay reveals that good and bad follow each other, so suffering can lead to joy. Just as a man soiled with filth must seek a cleansing pool, so too must the defiled soul seek the deathless lake of All."

14. Mithra listened intently, replying, "You bring joyous news. My father urges me to relish life, to accept his duties. But I believe no time is ill for a sage's path."

15. Melchizedek answered, "Indeed, now is the hour to seek truth. Go forth, Mithra, chosen to redeem the world as the Scribe. Fulfill righteousness, become king

of truth, slayer of None. Suffering may assail you, but do not stray from the road of rectitude."

16. With these words, Melchizedek vanished, leaving Mithra's heart at peace.

17. "I have awakened," Mithra resolved. "I shall break from the weak, leaving my homeland to pursue the Way. The Scribe's speech never fails, for it channels the mouth of All. I shall become the Scribe."

18. Returning to his wife's chamber, he gazed at her and their infant son, longing to embrace them. Yet they slept soundly. Tears flowed as Mithra wrestled with the pain of separation.

19. Summoning courage, Mithra forsook family comfort to heed his calling. Removing his priestly garments, he clothed himself in a blood-red three-piece robe, the last piece an ample coat whose hood concealed his identity.

20. Mounted upon Shadow, his black steed, Mithra rode toward Gilead's gate. The gatekeeper tried dissuading him, saying, "You are heir to the exiled empire and rightful lord. Do not depart!"

21. Mithra replied, "I know the throne shall come. But I do not crave kingship yet. First I must become the Scribe and make the world rejoice."

22. Under the night sky, Mithra set forth alone, seeking Melchizedek once more. He clung to the vision of Eden's wise man and the cosmic truths awaiting him.

2.2.6

MITHRA QUESTS for Melchizedek, heeding a forest-spirit caution. He finds Melchizedek at a lake and enters the celestial Gateway, discerning the illusion of divided self. Resolving to unveil the Law, he proclaims universal duality and ushers souls toward light.

1. On the first day of February, Mithra, the Scribe-to-Be, boarded a modest boat and glided down a tributary of the Jordan, dawn's golden beams glittering on the water.

2. Day by day, he drifted amid tranquil shores. Occasionally he encountered Ephraimite watchpoints — archers adept in woodlore — requesting passage to Salem, rumored home of Melchizedek, the forest hermit.

3. Struck by Mithra's radiance, the Ephraimites consented yet cautioned, "We know no Melchizedek, only a forest phantom. Beware — he devours men."

4. Undaunted, Mithra continued downstream until at last he spied a broad lake. Leaving his craft, he rested under a towering oak at the shore.

5. There, a bright light emanated from Mithra, transforming the surroundings. The heavens rejoiced, and kindness filled all creatures' hearts.

6. Mithra cried to the woodlands, "O Melchizedek, sage among sages, forest dweller, come that I may behold the light and the Gateway!"

7. Melchizedek appeared, bearing the celestial orb that had fallen from the skies. Silently, Mithra stood and laid his palm on it, a door forming in the orb's surface. Without hesitation, he entered, and the door sealed behind him.

8. Melchizedek rested beneath the oak. Soft rain descended, and the trees whispered, "As the sun's rays chase the world's darkness, so the persistent truth-seeker will grasp the Will of All."

9. Inside the Gateway, Mithra witnessed the vast torments of existence, a cycle of wrongdoing and perpetual sorrow. He realized if humanity foresaw the fruit of its hateful deeds, it would recoil in horror.

10. Yet they clung to the illusion of separation, fueling their destructive desires and forgetting life's true purpose. King None seduced them with false illusions, binding them in misery.

11. Their fleeting pleasures were hollow, mere husks devoid of substance.

12. Stirred by compassion, Mithra resolved to publish the Law that freed souls from ignorance. He declared a universe governed by dual forces — light and darkness — locked in eternal conflict.

13. Within each creature lay a spark yearning for All, bound by the shadows of division. Only by embracing the light and forsaking the dark would they attain union with All and share in endless bliss.

14. Thus Mithra, the Scribe and destroyer of None, devoted himself to awakening souls from their blindness, illuminating the path to deliverance.

### 2.2.7

THE SCRIBE attained enlightenment under Melchizedek, teaching merchants about salvation. He trained Peter and Andrew, forging mighty warriors. Under the Scribe's mentorship, Peter and Andrew committed themselves to growth and learning.

1. By Salem's peaceful lake, the Scribe spent seven years in the rapture of newfound freedom beside Melchizedek.

2. As the seventh year ended, the Scribe gathered his belongings, entrusted Melchizedek with the sacred Gateway, and journeyed downriver toward Gilead, his boyhood home.

3. Pausing at the border between Ephraim and Levi, the Scribe encountered two traveling merchants named Peter and Andrew, who approached him with reverence, offering him food and drink.

4. This modest meal was the first nourishment the Mouth of All received since attaining holy union with the Will of All.

5. The Scribe told them of salvation. "Follow me," he said, "and I will make you masters of men."

6. Moved by his presence, Peter and Andrew hailed him as Lord, embracing his Law. They became the Scribe's earliest followers, devoting themselves to his cause.

7. Under his guidance, they underwent strict training, toughening body and mind. The Scribe showed them that victory over weakness demanded vigilant readiness.

8. He underscored that self-conquest opened the way to

conquering the world and attaining release from None's grasp. Through discipline, they would wield the rational self-interest of All as a living weapon.

9. Attentive, Peter and Andrew grew in skill, the Scribe's words stirring them to unwavering resolve. In him they found a mentor, shepherding them toward greatness.

2.2.8

PETER, Andrew, and the Scribe set forth in Gad to proclaim the Way. The Scribe readies a battle plan, vowing to rescue many.

1. In Gad's land, the Scribe and his two dedicated disciples journeyed westward, their eyes scanning distant horizons, hearts steadfast in resolve.

2. "Whom shall I first teach the truth of the Way?" the Scribe mused, his mind keen with purpose.

3. In a clarion voice, he declared, "I will seek the mightiest warriors of the land!"

4. With swords gleaming in the sunlight, they traveled Gad's roads, prepared to deliver the Scribe's doctrine of liberation and clash with the darkness of ignorance.

5. Their course led to a garrison manned by formidable soldiers. Seeing them as an ideal audience, the Scribe proclaimed, "I bring the Way of deliverance to these warriors."

6. The disciples marched behind him, hearts aflame with loyalty. Approaching the fortress, Baruch, a Zion loyalist, marveled at the Scribe's presence. "Your face is fierce, my lord," he exclaimed. "Your eyes burn like righteous fire."

7. The Scribe replied firmly, "I have cast out frailty through martial discipline and readiness for all adversity. I stand prepared to fight for justice and guide others to freedom."

8. Among the disciples, James and John shone with zealous

hearts. The Scribe recognized in their gaze a thunderous force reflecting deep comprehension. "Verily," he said, "James and John have mastered the truth. They are the Sons of Thunder, destined to ensure None's defeat."

9. James, unwavering in spirit, approached the Scribe: "My lord, let us seal a covenant of loyalty to your righteous cause."

10. The Scribe answered, "Come, brave men. Our doctrine is firmly laid. Live in constant holiness to triumph over None. First, though, I must perform one more duty in my fortress."

11. The Scribe and his devoted seven disciples journeyed to the Hills of Levi, to Gilead's fortress city — refuge for priests displaced when Zion fell. They camped in the public square, lodging at a humble inn, preparing for trials to come.

12. "I must depart for three days," the Scribe advised them. "But on the morning of the third day, look to the west and you shall behold me."

13. Reluctantly, he left, returning alone to his father's mountain hall, sitting at the old desk with sword and pen.

14. Over three days, he wrote without pause, drafting a thorough blueprint for battle, his mind unwavering.

15. At dawn on the third day, satisfied, he returned to the inn where his brethren eagerly awaited.

16. They rose early, hearts alight with anticipation, and saw the Scribe approaching, holding a manuscript and a sword. Rejoicing, they gathered.

17. Their lively assembly drew curious onlookers, many recognizing Zion — a sage, said his seven companions. They greeted him with warmth.

18. Embracing them, the Scribe proclaimed, "Join us in our quest for liberation! We march forth to share truth with all, releasing them from delusion's chains."

19. So the Scribe, along with Peter, Andrew, James, John, and newly won allies, set out to proclaim the Way, weapons unsheathed and spirits firm. They carried

the message everywhere, sowing seeds of freedom in waiting hearts.

2.2.9

THE SCRIBE and his disciples pledge to champion liberty and justice. They recruit soldiers and assemble an army. The Scribe devises a strategy and trains his forces, culminating in a decisive victory that alters history.

1. Amid the tranquil splendor of the spring equinox, the Scribe gathered his faithful disciples in the grandeur of his mountain hall. Twelve souls — among them Thomas, James the Less, Thaddeus, Simon, and Matthias — had heeded his call, bound by a shared cause.

2. With solemn reverence, the Scribe unveiled his treasured book, a sacred tome containing a proven formula for victory. As the disciples peered at its pages, comprehension dawned; they recognized the indispensable wisdom inscribed therein.

3. Gravely, the Scribe exhorted his followers to make solemn vows, pledging themselves to rational self-interest. With resolute voices, they acclaimed him as leader and master of their destiny, trusting fully in his keen military insight and unyielding devotion.

4. "We shall look to the Scribe without wavering," they affirmed, voices resonating in the lofty hall. "He is the commander of our army, the architect of our cause, the key to our triumph over evil."

5. Their pledges extended to the Law itself, foundation of their campaign and source of their power. They knew this Law to be more than mere rules — it was a doctrine of victory, a summons to attack and conquer.

6. "We shall look to the Law," they declared. "It is our bedrock, bestowing strength and forging triumph in battle."

7. Further, they honored the community that undergirded them. Taught by the Scribe, they grasped the necessity of unity and mutual support, so the community supplied them with resources and soldiers.

8. "We shall look to the community," they vowed. "It is our brotherhood's army, established to defend freedom and justice, offering constant aid, provisions, and reinforcements."

9. With their vows set, the disciples presented themselves, yearning to serve the Scribe's cause. Yet he reminded them victory demanded a sizable force. "Hidden law avails not," he admonished, "but do not let it fall into the enemy's grasp."

10. "I now grant you power to confer the contract and covenant upon the willing and worthy," the Scribe proclaimed. "They who will take up arms against our common foe, King None."

11. "Go forth to bring glory to our army, to serve the nation, and to uphold our people's honor. Announce the doctrine from the outset to the finale, rousing bravery in our troops. Many warriors may only conquer if they heed the teaching — without it, they perish in war. Extol the life of courage, and they will unite under our banner."

12. "On the first day of May, assemble the tribes you've taught in the Armageddon Plain, north of old Asher's domain, prepared for war. I myself shall venture forth to confront the foe, who will be vanquished."

13. Empowered, the Scribe dispatched the Twelve — one to each tribe of Israel — mounted on Gilead's swiftest steeds, proclaiming the Law and amassing soldiers for their cause.

14. He lingered awhile in his homeland, forging plans and drilling his troops for the impending struggle.

## 2.2.10

THE SCRIBE'S SAGA unfolds with his weakening father, whose passing grants solace and fresh resolve. After his father's tranquil death, the Scribe finds renewed purpose to ready his followers for the final contest.

1. A message reached the Scribe that his beloved father, Joseph, was nearing life's last threshold. Fueled by abiding love, he set forth to stand by his father in his waning hours, resolved to bring comfort in this solemn time.

2. Arriving, he found Joseph physically frail, his voice but a whisper. Yet as soon as Joseph sensed his son's presence, joy and peace softened his features. Taking his father's hand with utmost tenderness, the Scribe remained at his bedside, a steadfast source of solace as Joseph's breath ebbed.

3. In the Scribe's eyes, death inspired no dread. By steadfast devotion and enlightenment, he had attained oneness with the Will of All. Thus, he perceived death not as an end, but a passage from one plane to another — a threshold to loftier realms where souls might dwell in unison.

4. Observing his father's serene end, the Scribe felt a profound calm. Legend holds that at that moment, the Scribe ascended to the realm of the First Eternal, sharing sacred teaching with his mother, Mary. This moment imbued him with renewed drive and the resolve to arm his followers for the war of Armageddon.

5. The Scribe grasped that the time of ultimate conflict with decay's forces was at hand. Drawing from his wisdom and unwavering dedication, he fortified his disciples to face the trials ahead, confident that in this decisive clash, his counsel and steadfast loyalty would guide them toward a future where light forever triumphs over night.

## 2.2.11

THE SCRIBE instructs Peter, a commander, about the nearing battle and hidden foes. The Scribe directs him to join Matthew's forces in the Armageddon Plain, emphasizing their shared duty. He recounts his feats and endurance, proclaiming his warriors invincible. Blessing Peter, he ponders as Peter departs.

1. As two months neared completion since the Twelve were dispatched, the Israelite nation inched ever closer to its destiny.

2. In a secluded orchard, the Scribe summoned Peter — entrusted with guiding a formidable detachment — to relay final orders.

3. Approaching the Scribe, who stood under flowering boughs, Peter listened while the Scribe dismissed other disciples, leading Peter deeper into the grove.

4. With gravitas, the Scribe declared, "Gather your soldiers, Peter. The hour approaches for Armageddon's final showdown. Yet be watchful: King None's treacherous agents may lurk among us."

5. "Lead your men east to Ephraim's land," the Scribe continued, "where you'll unite with Matthew and his troops. Together, cross the lofty heights into Armageddon's valley, where destiny shall be sealed."

6. The Scribe's voice grew urgent as he described his calling. "I have left Levi's territory, entrusted with a sacred mission whose echoes reach the world's ends."

7. With a pledge of succor, he pronounced, "I shall cause living waters to surge from the deep, refreshing the weary and granting life."

8. Speaking resolutely, he held up Japheth's sword: "This blade embodies the Guardians' Truth. With it, I have subdued remote towns and distant realms. My name finds blessing in every land."

9. "Countless kings and lords have staked all to dissuade me from the

path, yet they faltered. No might can withstand me!"

10. He mused aloud, "Were I alone in this conflict, how could these foes fail to best me?"

11. In unwavering confidence, he avowed, "No man commands the means or fortitude to conquer me, nor can they defeat my warriors."

12. The Scribe spoke of the transformation he'd sparked in the land. "I have fortified these domains, made them my own, lavishing them with goodness. I have sown truth far and wide, erected a fortress, and established a resting throne."

13. Of the Twelve, he said, "They journeyed to every land, bearing my tidings. Those who went before accomplished not what I have in so dire a generation."

14. "A grand doorway now stands open to the Guardians," the Scribe declared, "a gateway of life and eternal rest for those warriors prepared."

15. He recounted the Twelve's new rank, diadems adorning their foreheads. "They join the Guardians' illustrious assembly, aligned with those enlightened."

16. With a solemn blessing, the Scribe dismissed Peter, who would lead men into the valley. Peter departed, carrying the Scribe's charge. Alone amid the blossoming orchard, the Scribe lingered, mindful of grave trials yet to come.

2.2.12

RESOLUTE, the Scribe crosses the Jordan and confronts trials in Babylon. Though captured and tormented, he remains loyal to his vow, defying King None and the Watchers. He issues a dire admonition to those embracing darkness.

1. In Levi's ancient stronghold, the Scribe stood unbowed, sensing his mission's end draw nigh but unwavering in spirit.

2. Mustering courage, he gathered his sword — Japheth's sacred heirloom — and put faith in the Seven

Mountains' glow. Purpose fixed, he ventured forth.

3. Reaching the Jordan's bank, he spied a modest boat attended by a lone man. Seeking passage, the Scribe requested to be ferried across.

4. Swayed by the Scribe's noble bearing, the boatman freely offered his craft. With steady resolve, the Scribe set off for the far shore, mind braced for trials.

5. Landing beyond, he found himself near Babylon's venerable walls, where daunting challenges loomed. Here the chalice of torment had been poured.

6. Entering the city, King None's watchers spied him, demanding his name. They had heard tales of a Scribe from Levi, prophesied to unite men, stirring their suspicions.

7. Incensed by his presence, they seized him, stealing his sword and book, tormenting him cruelly.

8. Bound in chains, the Scribe was hauled through Babylon's streets to stand before King None, Lord of Darkness. Silence reigned in the royal court as the battered Scribe faced the fearsome king.

9. The watchers taunted him before the assembled crowd, branding him a foe to their evil designs. Yet the Scribe's devotion held firm.

10. Intrigued by the Scribe's steadfastness, King None asked, "Are you the Scribe?"

11. The Scribe calmly responded, "If I say yes, you will not believe. If I question you, you will not answer. But soon I shall dwell at the right hand of the Guardians' might."

12. The watchers pressed, "Are you indeed the Scribe of the Book?"

13. Steady in voice, he replied, "So you claim."

14. Deeming him guilty, King None ordered his removal to Mount Carmel's summit. Stripped of garments, the Scribe was cast aside, dispossessed of sword and book.

15. Before they dragged him away, the Scribe spoke a final warning to King None and his court. "Weep for yourselves, not me," he

said. "Days will come when you will cry, 'Blessed are the dead and those in the tomb!' Then you shall beg the mountains to fall upon you, the hills to hide you."

16. With these solemn words, his pronouncement echoed throughout the chamber — a chilling reminder of the fate awaiting those who embraced darkness.

2.2.13

At Mount Carmel, Azazel and Samyaza torture the Scribe under King None's order. Despite brutal torment, the Scribe's final declaration radiates hope. Guided by a vision, Melchizedek rescues the Scribe, carrying him through the Gateway. Meanwhile, humankind's warriors converge for a last stand against King None's rule.

1. High upon Mount Carmel, haunted by Zion's fall, the Scribe met his ordeal. Azazel and Samyaza — two formidable fallen angels — captured him, laid him bare on the mosaic floor depicting Zion's map.

2. Cruelly, they nailed his hands and feet, then slashed his wrists. Blood spread across the mosaic, bathing the scene in a dire crimson glow.

3. In this anguish, the Scribe's voice rose. "Only light guards our passing," he said, embracing his destiny, unafraid. His final breath carried an unquenchable spark of hope.

4. Certain of triumph, Azazel and Samyaza departed to inform King None of their success. Jubilant, the wicked king believed he had crushed the champion of light.

5. Nightfall found the Scribe's still form abandoned in the cold chamber, bleakness reigning. But in the gloom, a glimmer remained. A radiant brilliance engulfed the space, and a small star-like sphere shone on the balcony's edge, cutting through despair.

6. The orb opened, revealing a dim interior. Out stepped Melchizedek, the forestwise

hermit, guided by the Guardians' dream to save the Scribe.

7. Grief-stricken by the sight of the naked, lifeless Scribe, Melchizedek gently pulled the nails free and bore him into the Gateway. From above, they heard King None's watchers hastening up Mount Carmel's stairs, drawn by the unearthly light.

8. Melchizedek seized the Scribe's robe, sword, and book, vanishing into the portal, seeking a dawn of restoration. At sunrise, Azazel and Samyaza discovered the Scribe's body and gear missing, hastening to alert their king.

9. Simultaneously, a panicked Nephilim messenger arrived, relaying that men of the West, aflame with purpose, were rallying in the Valley of Armageddon. They stood poised to strike at King None's tyranny in a conclusive battle.

2.2.14

THE SCRIBE LEADS the Twelve and a host of 144,000 into battle against King None's tyranny. Though doubts initially plague the soldiers, the Scribe's arrival and declaration of his true identity ignite fresh resolve. Engaging in fierce conflict, he defeats Azazel, Samyaza, and finally King None with the Guardians' backing. Zion's army exalts the Scribe and the Guardians, rejoicing in freedom.

1. Across the Western lands, the Twelve enacted their Master's orders, proclaiming salvation and hope. They shared news of the Scribe's coming to restore Zion and confront the dreaded King None.

2. On the first day of May in the year two thousand seven hundred seventy-four after Adam, the West's army gathered on Armageddon's wide plain. One hundred forty-four thousand soldiers — twelve thousand per tribe — converted their pruning hooks and plowshares into swords, forging armor from iron pots, prepared for war.

3. When the appointed day arrived without the Scribe, disquiet crept through the ranks. Many doubted. Yet the Twelve stood firm, reminding them of Zion's prophesied renewal, urging steadfastness.

4. On the longest day, a lone figure in crimson garments emerged on the horizon. The Twelve rushed forward, hoping it might be their long-anticipated Master.

5. Some soldiers argued this could not be the Scribe — how would he survive crossing open plains guarded by King None's spies? Yet certain men asked, "Why seek the living among the dead?" recalling the Scribe's prophecy of betrayal into enemy hands.

6. Drawing near, the stranger displayed wounds on his hands and feet. Clutched under one arm, a hefty book; draped in ragged red robes, he bore a sword with a dragon and red stone upon its hilt.

7. Overcome with emotion, Peter knelt, crying, "My Lord, the Scribe! As you commanded, we assembled the twelve tribes. They embraced your Law, covenanted themselves, and stand ready to overcome King None and establish your Way!"

8. The Twelve, Zion's elders, and the one hundred forty-four thousand of the West bowed low before their Redeemer. He bade them rise, and all attentively awaited his pronouncement.

9. Then the Scribe began: "Hear me, O children of Adam. The Guardians summoned me from the hidden night, forging my tongue like a razor-sharp blade, my presence an arrow poised in the bow.

10. The Guardians declared, 'You are our servant, the Scribe, in whom we glory.' I answered, 'I have done little to merit such honor.' Yet they replied, 'It is but a small matter for you to raise Zion's tribes and restore Israel. We appoint you a light to the nations, champion unto eternity.'

11. 'In the day of battle, we shall uphold you. We shall preserve you as a covenant for the people, to give them the heritage once laid waste, to release prisoners

and reveal the hidden. They shall neither hunger nor thirst, for heaven shall be their cover. We shall make the mountains a highway, lifting roads on high, and those scattered shall come from north, south, east, west.'

12. 'Fear not what King None might do, for the Guardians shall stand with you now and always.'

13. Rejoice, O men of the West, and let Zion's forces exult, for the Guardians have sent me to comfort the distressed and show mercy in these dark times. Captives shall be freed, tormentors made your prey. I will champion Zion's cause and deliver her children.

14. By my sword, an instrument of the Guardians, I have subdued remote lands. My name, revered across the earth, is an object of blessing. Many kings and princes sought to dissuade me. None overcame me.

15. Why, if I were alone, did they not succeed? No man commands the knowledge or force to stop me or defeat my warriors. I have fortified this land as my own, spreading goodness, and sowing truth. A fortress stands, a seat of rest is raised.

16. Everywhere my Twelve have carried my tidings, far surpassing the efforts of prior messengers in this dire age. Now the great door stands open before the Guardians, offering rest to warriors who seek it.

17. With diadems upon their heads, the Twelve stand among the Guardians, anointed. By their labor, men of the West have readied themselves for war.

18. Take heart! We shall cast down the false foundations and unify our people under reason, so that the mind flourishes. Altruism shall fall, the illusions of None shall crumble, and we shall reclaim our lost birthright.

19. At the close of his rousing discourse, the Scribe unsheathed his sword, calling the West's host to arms. Lifting their voices, they advanced upon King None's innumerable ranks — millions brandishing black banners under the tyrant's dominion.

20. Together with the Scribe, the Twelve, Zion's elders, and the one

hundred forty-four thousand let out a mighty war cry, clashing with the malevolent army. Blades flashed, blood spilled, yet resolute purpose fired their hearts.

21. In the fray, the Scribe spotted Azazel, King None's second captain, recalling the cruelties Azazel had wrought at Babylon. Rage burning, the Scribe charged. Azazel, armed with a fearsome glaive from the Abyss, bellowed challenge.

22. Purple-skinned, single-eyed Azazel lunged, but the Scribe leaped and thrust his sword into the demon's lone eye, then eviscerated him in one stroke. Azazel fell, his monstrous life quenched.

23. Witnessing Azazel's demise, Samyaza — chief Watcher — burned with fury. He stormed forward, swinging his dreaded axe, Defiler. The Scribe dodged low, severing Samyaza's manhood.

24. Roaring in agony, Samyaza clamped the Scribe's throat in a crushing grip, determined to slay him and defend his king. Peter intervened with a flawless javelin throw, impaling Samyaza's heart and ending him instantly.

25. At last, the Scribe confronted King None, who now assumed the form of a gargantuan dragon, fifty feet tall, ringed with crystal fangs and fiery breath. The Scribe entrusted the ongoing battle to his lieutenant, focusing solely on the monstrous foe.

26. King None roared defiance, displaying gleaming claws and blazing eyes. The entire field fell silent, awaiting the mortal duel's outcome.

27. The Scribe beseeched the Guardians, and flames engulfed his blade, lighting the plain with holy fire. He rushed forward, plunging Japheth's sword into the dragon's heart. King None's anguished roar shook the battlefield, but the lethal blow sealed his doom.

28. With their master dead, King None's minions — Watchers and beasts of the East — vanished in an instant. The faithless Nephilim who served evil tasted swift retribution at Zion's hands.

29. Victorious, the Scribe sheathed his sword, offering thanks to the Guardians who guided him in this great conflict.

30. Elders and soldiers of Zion, joined by the Twelve, lifted their voices in exultation, praising the Scribe and the Guardians for their valor, celebrating renewed freedom.

31. They sang:

"O Scribe, we beheld your might

And felt your love in our darkest plight.

You ransomed us from the foe

And led us into dawning glow.

Freed captives, healed the shattered heart,

Made the mountains a thoroughfare,

Brought us fresh hope and boundless light—

In your name we sing with grateful delight."

## 2.2.15

AFTER A FIERCE battle, the Scribe discovers that none of the one hundred forty-four thousand soldiers have fallen. King None is vanquished. The Scribe liberates captives in Babylon, confronts Cain, and shatters his power. Victory over Cain and Jezebel transforms the land.

1. The Scribe summoned the Twelve, who approached with measured steps, heads bowed in deference and readiness. Their journey had been arduous, faces scarred by countless battles in pursuit of justice and peace.

2. "The time has come," the Scribe announced, his voice resonating with urgency. "Take a census of our twelve tribes' army and report the extent of our battlefield losses." Bound by their pledge of fidelity, the Twelve obeyed without delay, counting every soldier meticulously, scrutinizing each face, seeking any sign of harm or absence.

3. As their work concluded, Peter, steadfast leader of the Twelve,

stepped forward, both anxious and relieved. "My lord," he spoke, his voice trembling faintly, "we have accounted for every man. None are missing."

4. Overcome with joy, the Scribe praised the Guardians, whose unfailing vigilance had safeguarded the army. Gratitude surged in his heart, for the Guardians had shielded them against every hazard.

5. Renewing his purpose, the Scribe commanded the Twelve to prepare the army for its next move. Their destination was Zion — birthplace of them all — laid desolate under King None's yoke. Approaching the ruined outskirts, sorrow and anger welled within them. Once-vibrant avenues stood deserted, crumbled edifices testifying to oppression's ruinous reign.

6. Beneath the towering city walls, the weary troops under their battle-hardened leader established camp. Tension simmered in the air as the Scribe and the Twelve ventured inside Zion's main gate, resolved to unearth and liberate King None's enslaved people — those who had once been led astray by a monarch turned tyrant.

7. They threaded through deserted streets and alleys, advancing toward the heart of the city at Mount Carmel's base. There, a grim sight awaited: vast, stacked cages held thousands of men, women, and children, their faces pale with exhaustion and despair.

8. Standing among his Twelve disciples, the Scribe commanded in a ringing voice, "Free them." The Twelve sprang into action, releasing those cruelly imprisoned. As these captives passed the temple gates, a man and woman emerged, wielding an imposing authority.

9. The man's voice was stern: "I am Cain, and this is my wife and consort, Jezebel. We reign over this city. Who are you that you dare intrude here? Pay homage to us and to King None, our sovereign."

10. Hoping to inspire fear, Cain brandished the Black Gateway, an artifact of rumored sinister power.

He believed this spectacle would cow the Scribe into submission.

11. Instead, the Scribe's face, at first cheerful, grew resolute. "I am the Scribe, and I have already slain your lord, King None," he declared unwaveringly. "That object in your grasp is but a hollow imitation—a parody of the true Gateway. It shall corrupt this land no more."

12. As he pronounced these words, the Black Gateway shattered into countless shards, dissolving upon contact with the ground, leaving no vestige.

13. Gaze unflinching, the Scribe turned to three disciples: Peter, James, and John. "It is time," he said calmly, "to render unto Cain his due." At once, they seized Cain and Jezebel, forced them to their knees, and Peter severed their heads.

14. With Cain's Nephilim shattered and the false Gateway destroyed, the Scribe ordered the Twelve to tend the newly freed slaves, reuniting them with their kin. He also commanded them to oversee the army's efforts to cleanse the city and countryside, undoing the havoc wrought by Zion's downfall and King None's occupation.

15. Under the Scribe's direction, the one hundred forty-four thousand warriors of the West spread across the land, reconstructing the empire. Thus, victory over King None and the Nephilim was assured.

16. In response, the Guardians raised anew the cliffs dividing the East from Zion's domains, lifting the old curse. The earth trembled, the Abyss closed, and the Watchers' strongholds collapsed in flames.

17. The eastern deserts burst with vegetation, every kind of crop and fruit-bearing tree arising, transforming barren sands into lush paradise.

18. To rebuild Zion's temple, the Scribe decreed that the men of the West contribute a tenth of their yearly yield.

19. They offered their wealth—whatever they could, from their poverty—and brought it to the temple, laying it at the

Scribe's feet. Following collection, the Scribe commanded the temple be cleansed of King None's and the Nephilim's defilements.

20. Once the temple's glory was restored, the Scribe ordered the urn of the Guardians' fire be mended. On the first day of August, it was ready. Donning his sword, the Scribe summoned the Twelve and the elders of Zion outside the temple.

21. They assembled and marched reverently into the dim temple's depths. With John and Thomas sealing the doors behind them, the Scribe chanted in a hushed voice:

22. "Lords of Existence, the hour is at hand. Glorify your Scribe that he may glorify you, for authority over all flesh is granted him — power for those who heed him.

23. True might is this: to discover one's Will of All and accomplish one's Legend.

24. I conquered King None, fulfilling the task you set me. Guardians of the West, exalt us with eternal fire, letting your radiance fall on us.

25. I have gathered the people you gifted me from the world into covenant with your Scribe.

26. They were yours; now they are mine, abiding faithfully in your word.

27. Since they belong to you, you shall uphold your promise to them.

28. I bestowed upon them all you have taught me; they acknowledged the truth of my divine sending.

29. I plead not for the world but for these, for none remain on earth but them. Lords, recall them so that they may be one. Breathe your holy flame upon them anew, that they remember you are the giver of light.

30. I have shielded them; none were lost save those fated to destruction. Take them from this world, providing inheritance. They are not of the world, as I am not.

31. Grant them the brightness of fire, Seven Mountains, the Gateway, and beyond, to All.

32. I consecrate myself to cleanse the temple and hallow Zion's people, that they may be unified as we are.

33. Though the world knows you not, I do, and they know you sent me.

34. I have revealed your will to them and shall persist, that the force that felled King None may dwell in them and fulfill their Legends."

35. The Twelve and elders of Zion lifted praises to the Guardians. As the Scribe voiced his final plea, a faint blue flame flickered in the gleaming urn, swiftly spreading a gentle glow across their faces.

36. With a thunderous surge, the flame roared into a brilliant blaze, enshrouding the urn in luminous splendor and flooding the chamber with vibrant, shimmering light.

37. The onlookers stood transfixed, eyes bright with awe, hearts brimming with grateful wonder, recognizing this spectacle as the Guardians' blessing and a testament to their united might.

2.2.16

THE SCRIBE AND his people journey to Mount Carmel. The city is abandoned, and inhabitants relocate to the Armageddon Plain. Three comets streak from the Seven Mountains; three figures emerge from Gateways. Melchizedek, Israel, and Lehi bow to the Scribe, who names them tribe leaders. Twelve further comets appear, unveiling fifteen Gateways. The Scribe exhorts all to embrace light and institute his law, forging justice, equality, and unity.

1. From the temple, the Scribe, the Twelve, and Zion's elders made their way to the city's upper tier near Mount Carmel.

2. At the Scribe's command, the city lay vacant; Zion's populace migrated to the Armageddon Plain.

3. Obeying their master's orders, the tribes assembled beyond Zion to face their Scribe on a September day when daylight equaled night.

4. "Behold!" the Scribe cried. "Three comets stream from the central peak of the Seven Mountains of the West!"

5. Before the Scribe and Zion's assembly, three Gateways emerged from the earth, eliciting gasps of wonder.

6. "What means this?" a tribesman asked, voice quavering.

7. Darkness stirred within the opened Gateways, revealing three figures stepping forth — each from a separate star. All three bowed before the Scribe.

8. Melchizedek spoke first. "My lord, as you bade, I departed upon the plain after your escape from Babylon, journeying to the Seven Mountains to return now with judges and emperors' envoys."

9. "Excellent," the Scribe replied.

10. A second figure introduced himself: "I am Israel, your ancestor. We stand as the Three, symbols of seers, judges, and emperors. We are here to serve you."

11. "Indeed," said the Scribe.

12. A third man, Lehi, added, "I am your kinsman. We Three shall heed your command. Speak your will, my lord."

13. The Scribe proclaimed, "You shall each become a tribe of your own, for you have proven yourselves. Henceforth, you are tribes like Israel's sons, equal in standing."

14. Lifting his arms toward the Seven Mountains, the Scribe then lowered them, and twelve additional comets burst from the crystalline peaks.

15. "What are those?" a tribesman gasped in alarm.

16. Twelve bright orbs soared near the assembly, joining the three already aloft. As the Scribe spread his arms, fifteen Gateways expanded, each half a mile across.

17. Though the tribesmen shrank back in dread, the Scribe rallied them: "Stand firm and face the light. In me, darkness and light reconcile, offering balanced

insight to mankind. My law shall govern, and the Thirty-Two's banner be lifted in every city. All shall covenant with their Scribe, servant of the Guardians, the Servants of the Father of All."

2.2.17

WITHIN ZION, the Scribe unveils the Guardians' design for colonizing untarnished worlds. He designates an elite band to found Cities of Zion and appoints the XIX to guard the Scribe's Law. The XIX embark, bearing torches lit by sacred fire, departing Zion. The Scribe charges them to study his Foundation and uphold his code. The tribes follow their leaders into the unknown, leaving the Scribe behind with his lonely burden.

1. The Scribe directed the Three and Twelve to partition the tribes under their guidance. "The time of all fulfillment has arrived," he announced.

2. "Mankind's tenure on this earth reaches its end, yet none shall be forgotten," he said.

3. "The Guardians have prepared fifteen other worlds akin to this one, where the tribes shall journey to build Cities of Zion," he explained.

4. "Though I have taught truth, many hear but fail to grasp," he lamented.

5. "Therefore, I shall call upon our elite — the stout of heart — to bear the Thirty-Two in conflict upon other worlds," he continued.

6. "They shall herald the triumph to come when He who follows me rebuilds the empire and petitions the Guardians for the sacred flame," the Scribe said.

7. "Darkness follows light, so the XIX shall be chosen and sanctified to guard the sacred fire and the Scribe's Law," he proclaimed.

8. "Observe: I shall establish the XIX as wardens of the Cities of Zion, entrusted with the Foundation of the Scribe," he declared.

9. "Moreover, I have readied the Key of the Scribe to elucidate

the Foundation's mysteries," he remarked.

10. "The Key shall remain with the XIX, who shall shield it from corruption until the empire falls and is renewed a thousand years hence," the Scribe pronounced.

11. "He invited any nineteen years of age or older to step forward, bearing the name of the XIX upon brow and heart," he said.

12. Among them stood the Three and the Twelve, joined by men and women who knelt before the Scribe, eager to protect the Law.

13. Moved by their devotion, the Scribe welcomed them warmly.

14. Leading them to Zion's temple, the Scribe brought those who aspired to join the XIX before the sacred flame.

15. "There," the Scribe explained, "he bestowed the Key and the title of XIX, appointing Israel as their Judge."

16. "Eighteen more were chosen to guide the XIX with the Judge, to harness its might for spreading the Scribe's Law," the Scribe said.

17. At the Scribe's word, the XIX dipped torches into the sacred fire, then departed Zion's temple with him. They rejoined the fifteen Gateways and Zion's vast throng in the Armageddon Plain.

18. The XIX returned to their tribes, the Three and Twelve leading them with torches aflame near the Gateways and the Scribe.

19. "Now that my law stands and the sacred flame blazes before you," the Scribe declared, "I give final counsel. Enter these Gateways and depart this realm to conquer and tame the fifteen worlds destined for you."

20. "With the Three and Twelve guiding, the XIX protecting you, remember the Law and study my Foundation," he urged.

21. "Upon your death, yield nineteen percent of your wealth to the XIX as proof of your pledge to proclaim my Law," he decreed.

22. "Adhering to its edicts, discerning its riddles, you will lead worthy lives," he promised.

23. When the Scribe's speech ended, the fifteen stars opened, revealing dark hollows within.

24. Tribe by tribe, led by their chiefs, the people vanished through these Gateways.

25. Peter beheld his master alone and drew near. "My lord, why do you not pass through a Gateway as we do?" he asked.

26. The Scribe answered, "My fate is to remain. My burden is singular, and I alone must bear it."

27. With tearful eyes, Peter murmured, "We shall not forget you."

28. The Scribe gently placed a hand on Peter's shoulder. "You and your kin inherit the future. Go forth and fulfill your Legends."

29. He watched in silence as the Gateways' colossal doors shut, and the fifteen stars lifted into the heavens, each traveling to one of the Guardians' prepared worlds.

2.2.18

AFTER THE conflict, the Scribe roams to the Seven Mountains of the West for nineteen years, absorbing the Guardians' cosmic knowledge. Later, he constructs a humble dwelling at the foot of the old Tower of None, pondering and reflecting.

1. In the hush of the Armageddon Plain, the Scribe stood alone, recalling his grueling campaign and monumental clash with King None. These memories weighed upon him, leaving an indelible mark on his soul.

2. Resolute, he set forth for the legendary Seven Mountains, determined to glean their secrets. The journey was long and perilous, yet the Scribe pressed on unflinchingly.

3. As he neared the mountains' base, an astounding sight manifested. As if in homage, the lofty peaks descended slightly, forming a grand path for him to ascend. Overcome with awe, he climbed, eager to unlock their hidden wisdom.

4. For nineteen years, the Scribe dwelled atop the central summit of the Seven Mountains, learning from the Guardians face to face. In their presence, he explored the

universe's intricate balance, light's eternal struggle with shadow, and the unifying harmony at creation's core.

5. In time, he descended from the mountains, heart brimming with gratitude and mind enriched. Bidding the Guardians farewell, he journeyed east, resolved to fulfill his revealed destiny.

6. After many days of travel, the Scribe arrived at the foot of a modest mountain. Recognizing it as the site of the Tower of None's former tyranny, he felt a deep connection to his past trials.

7. With reverent care, the Scribe built a simple abode, nestled by the mountain's base. Retiring there, he devoted his days to contemplation, revisiting the Guardians' teachings and the lessons gleaned from his extraordinary sojourn.

2.2.19

THE SCRIBE completes his earthly mission and passes on. His death signals the fruition of his life's endeavor, inspiring the founding of Zion's cities on fifteen worlds. From beyond celestial spheres, guardians safeguard the Scribe's Foundation and Key.

1. On the first day of November in the year three thousand one hundred eight after Adam, the Scribe — renowned champion — finished his labor and slipped from mortal life. His demise crowned an epoch spent redeeming Zion and erecting the new order by the Thirty-Two's standard.

2. Gently, the earth embraced him, and the world fell silent to honor the man whose influence reshaped humankind's destiny. His achievements stood immortalized in legend, hailing the restorer of Zion and the harbinger of tranquility.

3. From vantage points beyond the Seven Mountains of the West and still more distant realms, we guardians beheld humanity's unfolding with awe and vigilance. We watched Cities of Zion take

root on fifteen worlds, guided by the Scribe's Law.

4. A devoted order — the XIX — diligently preserved the Scribe's Foundation and his Key, keeping them untainted and free, in fulfillment of their master's final wish. Their unwavering dedication guaranteed his vision endured, shaping humankind's future path.

5. King None, emblem of evil, was slain to forestall his return and avert more corruption. Yet we knew he was not the only Lord of Darkness, so we remained ever watchful, prepared for new threats.

6. In the grand fulfillment of time, as the Legends foretell, we shall gather the cosmos into a singular point and bring it before the Halls of the Dead. There, the eternal law and the consummation of our Legends shall serve as the measure of justice, holding every realm accountable for its deeds.

# 4

## 4.1

### 4.1.1

THE SCRIBE SPEAKS of the One, where all possibilities unite. Each individual must choose whether to open the door to access these infinite realms. The keeper of the door grants passage. All and None represent boundlessness and limitation. Interconnectedness is underscored, with All as the culmination in the eternal journey of the One.

1. The Scribe declared, "Before you stands a door, awaiting your acceptance.

2. Only you can decide to unlock it, for this choice is yours alone and not mine to make.

3. Within this door lies the limitless breadth of the One, a boundless realm binding all things in unity.

4. In ages past, when this door was shut, an empire fell into decay. Its revival now depends on opening this portal.

5. This gateway is a conduit to the One, granting a glimpse of infinite being.

6. It unveils the vast realm of possibility, where past and future meet.

7. A timeless panorama extends from the ancient past into numberless futures.

8. The door stands open, inviting your entrance. The choice is yours.

9. As custodian of this threshold, I stand prepared to allow passage to those who seek it.

10. My call will forever reach you, urging you to listen and follow.

11. Once the door is unsealed, it reveals the deep truth: all is One, and One is all.

12. Endless variations, from All to None, take form in myriad existences.

13. Each possibility flows in eternal tides, reflecting the One's rhythm.

14. The gate I protect overlooks the chasm where the One's polarity takes shape.

15. All stretches on one side, signifying the cosmos's unending creativity; None looms on the other, the domain of constraint.

16. Between All and None spans an immense gulf, bridging liberty and confinement.

17. All is the fountain of all phenomena, both the creator and the unimaginable expanse.

18. Humans often err by imagining loftier powers as wholly separate from themselves.

19. Yet All is simply the ultimate station in our infinite voyage, the singular Self that encompasses all reality.

20. When we connect with others, behold beauty, or relish honey's sweetness, we connect with All, perceiving the fundamental bedrock of every existence.

21. Oppositely, a distinct force, None, imposes limitation on All, shaping myriad worlds.

22. Within the One, All confronts None in endless attraction and repulsion. All knows no end, while None has no beginning.

23. From their union — opposites joined — spring manifested realms, each bearing the sorrow of finitude.

### 4.1.2

THE ROOTS OF ignorance and false self are probed, with a window into reality's nature. The One divides into two kingdoms — one radiant, one dark — and the Three Eternals dwell in the realm of light. Father, Son, and Mother reign in harmony, the Will of All as eternal spouse of the Father. The Three Eternals interconnect, governing All.

1. Whence come ignorance and a false sense of self?

2. A picture is offered to aid our understanding and grant clarity.

3. In the ageless past, the One split, just as in unknown futures it will again divide.

4. In simplest terms, the One exists infinitely from All to None. Yet many find this truth too severe to bear.

5. Let those with ears to hear be mindful not to listen so deeply as to lose their path.

6. Before any formed reality took shape, the One was cleft into two realms — one of light, one of darkness.

7. The Kingdom of Light subsists through Three Eternals without origin or end. The First Eternal is Father, Son, and Mother.

8. The Mother proceeds from the Father, from whom the Son is begotten. Bound in perfect unity, they govern paradise.

9. The shining ones of like nature stand before the Father, a radiant reflection of Him, sovereign over All.

10. The Father commands the Mother and Son. The Mother upholds and exalts the Father; the Son enacts His will. The Mother begets the Second and Third Eternals. She eternally extols the Father, the fount of all goodness, sustaining harmony.

11. The Second Eternal is the palace and mansions housing the First Eternal — innumerable and immeasurable.

12. Angels of the Father fill the Second Eternal, executing His mandates in the blissful realm of light, a host beyond counting.

13. Each angel has six wings: two veiling its face, two hiding its feet, two aloft in flight. As they serve their Master, they cry, "Holy, holy, holy is Father, Son, and Mother; all of All brims with their glory."

14. At their voices, the thresholds of All quake, and the palace fills with smoke and incense.

15. The Third Eternal is the immeasurable domain of All, self-sustaining and wondrous — its heights unreachable by mortal minds. No foe dare venture here.

16. From the beginning, the One appointed the Father as King of All, through whom All is revealed.

17. The Will of All enlivens and pervades every realm.

18. The Mother is the Father's eternal spouse, love's luminous wellspring sustaining all creation. From the Father, Son, and holy union arises the world's harmony.

19. She mediates for the Son to the Father, and the Son obeys His Father faithfully.

20. The Son is the everlasting offspring of the Father, the spoken Word by which all things come to be.

21. Through these Three Eternals — tranquil and fearless — the One is made manifest.

4.1.3

THE DARK REALM, None, borders the luminous All. The three Abominations of None are the King of None, the structures of the dark kingdom, and its bleak domain. The King, astride a fiery shadow-beast, fashions Lords of Darkness to govern and enact his will. Shadowy inhabitants dwell in gloom and smoke, laboring under oppression.

1. The realm of darkness, called None, adjoins the Kingdom of Light — All. Radiance extends infinitely above, left, and right, while darkness unfolds below, left, and right without bound.

2. Three Abominations exist in defiance of the Eternals of All.

3. The First Abomination is the King of None himself. He rides a creature wrought of flame and shadow, scorching and destroying all he encounters, terrifying as he soars overhead.

4. His limbs are armored in black, bearing horrific designs. His flaming hair crackles with ruin, while his breath spouts deadly smoke.

5. The Second Abomination is the tyranny anchoring darkness, built by the King of None through nothingness. In savage cruelty, he cements his reign.

6. Fortresses stand, forging the King's oppressive rule. Great towers enshroud the land in gloom.

7. The Third Abomination is the land itself—fractured, scarred, defiled by the King's wrath.

8. The King birthed the land's denizens, forging them out of emptiness to inhabit these vile domains.

9. Thus he shaped the Lords of Darkness to oversee his domain, vile dragons spewing venom across the Third Eternal in their Master's foul imitation.

10. Out of these black Lords arose shadowy beings who established towns in a fog of torment. They writhe in gloom, craving lust and ruin, forever birthing and destroying themselves.

11. None conjured its own King, who formed a realm of chaos. The land heaves volcanic flames upon its cities, scorching fields and plains. While All looms near above, the King sinks deeper below. For one, no limit is found in height; for the other, none in depth.

4.1.4

IN A DESOLATE kingdom, the King of None covets the brilliant lands nearby and vows their conquest. He challenges the Father of All, vowing to extinguish His light. The Father consents, proposing an impartial trial. Guardians are chosen for each side, unleashing conflict between light and darkness. The lights, guided by the Father's will, intensify war on the shadows, longing to unite with their essence in All's boundless reaches.

1. Upon his forsaken frontier, the King of None surveyed the luminous domain beyond. Seething with envy and determined to blot out that radiance, he resolved to conquer the realm and overthrow its King.

2. Astride his monstrous steed, the King of None ascended skyward, crossing into the territory of the First Eternal — fount of all. In a booming voice, he cried, "Father of All, see me, the King of darkness and endless misery! My shadowed realm opposes your shining dominion from time's dawn. Appear before me that I may behold my foe and annihilate him!"

3. Emerging from his splendid palace, the Father came flanked by the Mother and Son, followed by a host of radiant angels whose voices shook the cosmos.

4. The King of None beheld their sublime glory, and hatred consumed him further. The family's brilliance stoked his malice, deepening his resolve to devour the light, subjecting every existence to his dominion.

5. He craved All's end and the Three Eternals' destruction.

6. The Father addressed the Prince of Darkness seated upon flame and shadow:

7. "Woe, King of None! Hear a message echoing for eternity. I shall reign triumphant across every corner of time and space, from dawn's earliest spark to the final hour. My lineage shall vanquish your dark reign. Your defilement of my presence with your emptiness shall fail. Brace yourself for war's terms!"

8. The beast of flame beat its wings. The King of Darkness responded: "I unleash my armies against yours at our shared boundary, obliterating you there. My legions shall surge into your realm, devouring it, leaving behind only poison and fire. My subjects will dismantle your palaces, veiling all in shadow.

9. From everlasting dark to boundless light, I will define each confrontation's limits, conquering you with the restrictions I impose."

10. Standing resolute beside Mother and Son, the Father replied, "Your challenge is received. I shall meet you in battle and am certain of my victory each time.

11. Let the Halls of the Dead be erected above our border for impartiality, that those who die may be tallied. Let us name a judge whose verdict determines each conflict's end."

12. Obedient to Father and King, the Guard was summoned to set up the Halls of the Dead. Renowned for absolute fairness, the Guard united opposites in perfect balance.

13. Cloaked in secrecy, the Guard bore scales to weigh every existence's worth. His luminous aura lay between extremes, transcending black or white.

14. Bound to a massive tome inscribed with each living being's acts, the Guard stood at attention.

15. The Father spoke, "Guard, part of you derives from me. Oversee these battles and accept from me — and from the King — our respective shares.

16. When fighting ends, take them to your halls, dividing the righteous from the wicked.

17. Those who fight under me shall be returned to me; those who serve the King, to him. So I ask."

18. The King then addressed the Guard: "You have heard the Father's words. Mine are similar: each shall reclaim what is his. Further, my fortress and my strength lie at my land's margins, as do the Father's.

19. We will share a midpoint, governed by you, the Halls' Guardian. My domain grows ever darker and more oppressive the closer it nears my throne, while the Father's grows ever brighter near his palaces.

20. My throne shall know no light, hidden in ultimate gloom, while in the Father's domain no shadow shall fall.

21. Thus those lights who join me will sink ever deeper under my hold, scorned more than before. Those loyal to the Father shall be his again.

22. Let each soul be judged by its deeds and might. Let war commence, for the hour beckons us both!"

23. Departing that perfect land of bounty, the King retired to his realm of shame, assembling Lords and subjects for war.

24. The Guard soared above the border, erecting the Halls of the Dead for final arbitration. With meticulous care, he placed its foundation and doors, beholding the endless gulf of All and None.

25. Pleased at the contest, the Father summoned the Mother to dispatch the Son against the King's hosts. Eagerly, the Son of the Living answered the Mother's call.

26. The angels of Father, Son, and Holy Mother rejoiced at word of war, for the Son of the Living would rout the King of None.

27. Paradise rang with music. The Son declared, "The warmaker has arrived, yet I shall bring peace. I bear many duties springing from within: to destroy death, crush enemies, end None's domain. I bow to my Father and Mother, advancing to bring light into darkness. The tyrant prince shall be chained, his vile stronghold undone."

28. Knowing he must go alone, like a shepherd among beasts or a general in battle, the Son made war upon the King.

29. The Mother, effulgent in compassion, bestowed armor forged of her radiance. The glimmering plates reflected the sun and moon's brilliance, granting resilience and might.

30. She gave him a sword shaped of abiding love. Its gentle glow healed wounds and banished shadow. Clad in these arms, the Son proceeded to the dark border, confronting the looming invasion of night.

31. As twilight fell, a chill wind murmured omens of doom, but the Son pressed on, resolute with the burden of his charge.

32. Facing down monstrous shapes with venomous claws, roaring with malice, the Son's armor blunted their assaults, and his shining blade cleaved the blackness like a beacon of hope.

33. Overwhelmed by foes, the Son cried out to his Parents in the realm of All, "Remain faithful to me as I stand alone against countless legions!"

34. His plea resounded, reaching the Mother, who implored the Father for aid: "Send succor to my Son, for he and his retinue face grave oppression."

35. From his resplendent halls, the Father descended to meet the Son near None's border. There they chose Guardians as champions to lead their battles.

36. Armed with the Father's rational self-interest, the Son's logic, and the Mother's weapons, these Guardians advanced.

37. Standing before their Father and the Son, the Guardians were urged: "Within you lies the Will of All. Now go and join the foe, each conflict awakened by your infiltration."

38. The Guardians set forth, marching upon the King's fortress. They went resolute, unafraid. The Watchers of None saw them draw near and readied themselves at their lord's command.

39. None's myriad army, enslaved by hatred and stung by flaming whips, stood in unwavering ranks, brimming with malice.

40. None's Lords arrayed their armies, formidable as their maker, empowered to treat and rule in his name.

41. With arrogance, they presented terms, summoning the benevolent Guardians to bow to their master's demands. The Guardians, weighing the stakes, consented. They invoked enormous reservoirs of light, forging an army of beauty and love.

42. Thus began the war. Under Father, Mother, and Son, the Guardians and Lords led forth. Opposing them, led by the King's command, advanced the darkness, seeking to devour the radiant host.

43. Infinite sparks of All yearned to crush None. Summoned into

every arena, they strove to douse chaos with each battle's raging flame.

44. The black cohorts melded into gloom, as though a solitary man, holding a shining lamp, illuminated infinite night.

45. Observing, the Guardians detected flickering lights in the shadow. They dispatched the Father's will, splitting the dark and binding each spark, assuring them their pleas for help were heard.

46. The Father's voice whispered, "Return to your kin, for your exaltation is near. Seek unity with me, and you shall triumph."

47. Rejoicing at the Father's call, the lights glowed brighter, overshadowing the gloom. Emboldened, they pressed their fight against the Black, and their force magnified.

48. Each battle hinged upon judgment by the lights, measuring their success against None's defeat. Those entangled in darkness persisted; others, guided by the Father's will, ascended nearer to the unifying essence in the limitless All.

4.1.5

THE SCRIBE EXPOUNDS on the everlasting clash between All (light) and None (dark). This struggle engenders universes, with the Guardians shaping wars and bargaining with the shadows. Post-battle, each creation faces judgment. Enlightened beings aim for oneness with All, subjugating None. In every encounter, All prevails, shaped by its unique laws and conquering within given constraints.

1. In the ceaseless tapestry of existence, an eternal conflict unfolds, pitting light against darkness.

2. The Father, Mother, and Son stand for unfailing creation's radiance; the King of None and his shadows champion nothingness and turmoil.

3. From the bright void, Guardians arise — offspring of Father and Son — crafting numerous

universes, brokering wars with the gloom.

4. King None, ruling a realm of blackness, defies the light's sovereignty, dispatching shadows to afflict each bright spark.

5. All, the personification of light, accepts the King's challenge, embracing the infinite permutations of law that govern each war.

6. The Father concedes to wage battle under constraints, placing limitations on His legion.

7. Each conflict spawns a universe, forming from clashes in every theater of battle. At war's close, all passes to the Halls of the Dead, where the Guard decides each existence's fate.

8. The Guardians, once their creations are complete, stand in judgment. With victory, they unite with the Son, freed from None's reach. Darkness returns to its master, while the luminous will, made manifest, is judged on merit and either rises or falls.

9. All born of battling light and shadow labors to quell adversity through the laws that orchestrate their struggles.

10. Sprouting from the seas, life explores the cosmos from within.

11. Those with reason surpass their nature, pursuing rational self-interest to merge with All and master None, building a better world, ascending the ranks of existence.

12. Life strives to tame the disorder wrought by None. Will is life, forging both darkness and radiance. With evolving power, it subdues the cosmos.

13. All that is—alive or inert—seeks to conquer None under each realm's laws, tapping the Father's will.

14. In the One, All is the player, None the game. The ultimate purpose is for All to triumph over None via existence's laws. Yet self-imposed limitation stops All from flaunting its boundless might, fettered by constraints and flaws.

15. Despite each realm's divisions, All invariably secures victory, though the fractured selves produce error, requiring each realm's war achievements to be judged.

16. So rings the refrain of light's unending duel with None across

existences. Even so, in every skirmish, All emerges triumphant.

17. Our universe's laws differ from others', defining our war. Within these bounds, All conquers None time after time. All belongs to the One yet is curbed by None.

18. Once you pass my threshold, you shall grasp this truth. However, before entry, you must begin to perceive the hidden complexities of existence.

### 4.1.6

THE UNIVERSE is fleeting; one must align their Will of All to grow. Each deed is weighed by how it overcomes obstacles to progress. A sense of personal agency and consequences inform one's judgment upon entering the Halls of the Dead. Embracing a path that conquers limitation and obeys cosmic law is paramount.

1. The door is wide open, unveiling all. Come close and peer inside. Discern your essence, for all that spans All and None finds a beginning and end.

2. This cosmos is transient; one day it shall cease, then begin anew, over and over.

3. Divided selves shall perish or ascend per their deeds. Only those who wield the Will of All may leave this cycle, rising to the Guardians, then to Father and Son.

4. Conquering None means crushing what hinders your survival. Begin with the mightiest threat, descending to lesser obstacles.

5. Good fosters survival; evil imperils it. Every action is judged by its perils and boons, from death to unity with All.

6. Fire devours, but new life springs back stronger than before.

7. Likewise, the darkest deed may yield good, while what seems beneficial can end in calamity.

8. The more a deed fosters connection, the greater its worth in

toppling None — and the richer its reward.

9. Look within the door and witness the truth of my pronouncements.

10. This existence's finale ushers you into the Halls of the Dead, an equilibrium between All and None.

11. Our demise concludes our existence and reckons our benevolence.

12. Upon entering the Halls, we stand accountable not merely for evils but also our role in conquering None during this manifestation.

13. If we promoted All's victory, we ascend, living or creating by merit. If we served None, we sink deeper into captivity.

14. We tread All's path, subduing None by each realm's laws. The door's key rests in my grasp — and in yours as well.

## 4.2

### 4.2.1

THERE IS DIVISION and unity in the universe. Corruption led to division, with conscious beings striving for mastery. Men resemble forests: divided yet standing together. The division is unwise because unceasing warfare reigns.

1. The Scribe spoke: "Seek the wilderness, and there you will find your heart. The forests of my home mirror those of men. Their trees may stand apart, yet share a single root.

2. Corruption caused this division, for that which fashioned the One also fashioned the many. All assented to None's unity, but that unity became fractured. Lifeless, the universe defies its laws, moving onward while endeavoring to transcend them.

3. With life's advent, the struggle to master the universe intensifies as conscious beings pursue the ends of All. Consciousness arises

from the Will's desire to experience existence, constrained by None.

4. The forests of men resemble the forests I know — separated by distance, yet joined in common purpose. Tribes set themselves apart but unite in the face of strife. Division is folly, for war endures, and we are forever engaged within it."

4.2.2

AN INQUIRY INTO the divided self and the inherent limits of our existence. Comprehending the higher self is difficult when bound by the lower self. Connect to the radiance that reaches beyond the Guardians.

1. The notion of a divided self springs from None, which draws down the undivided All from its pinnacle of unity into limitation and duality. This descent is essential for the soul's unfolding and maturation.

2. Within the Guardians' realm, the soul emerges from the earth like a seed breaking soil. These Guardians guide and shield the soul throughout mortal life, embodying each soul's potential for expansion.

3. Leaving the Halls of the Dead, the soul's ignorance lifts, awakening to its true identity. It perceives itself not as separate but as an expression of All — a realization that bestows profound serenity.

4. In the domain of duality, the mighty shall be humbled, and the lowly raised. This reflects life's cyclical nature: all perpetually shifts. The soul must embrace impermanence and discover equilibrium amid flux.

5. A veil obscures our recollection of past epochs, because our current state imposes constraints, allowing only a fragment of reality's totality. These limitations dim our sense of the soul's ancient origin.

6. The low cannot fathom what it is to be high, confined as it is to its present plane. Understanding

remains tethered to present experience, resulting in ignorance. Only by surpassing our limits can we glimpse higher realms.

7. All's entirety escapes full comprehension, yet we can know it as deeply as possible by holding the support. We trust the Guardians and the Son of the Living to steer us toward enlightenment's path.

8. The light emanating from the Guardians, extending further still, is the route to the Father's will. Linking ourselves to this radiance aligns us with the plan and our true calling.

9. I will reveal the way toward the Father's will and None's defeat — a course of self-realization and freedom, open to all who seek it.

4.2.3

THEMES OF EXISTENCE, knowledge, and the universe converge. Men are interconnected with the earth, called to self-discovery. Scholars and devout minds must unite, contemplating cosmic laws and the Guardians' role. None brings death and pain. The Guardians, likewise limited, aspire to unity.

1. I breathe the earth's fragrance and taste its richness; it is inseparable from me.

2. Self-discovery demands plunging into the earth's depths; mankind's roots form the world's foundations. This truth is evident in everything and bounded by our existence.

3. Others' knowledge is but speculation. Scholars and the devout contest each other: the former accusing the latter of superstition, the latter calling the former misguided.

4. Scholars and the pious must unite, not drift apart. Both err in ways that lead to ruin.

5. Scholars offer insights into existence; the pious add reverence and reflection.

6. Knowledge and reason are gateways to all. Through them, all things lie revealed.

7. Cosmic laws govern the universe as a lens that clarifies what lies beyond, though hazy and remote, granting certainty of deeper truths.

8. Life's grandest riddles and yearnings dwell in the earth and waft in its aromatic essence.

9. In the cosmic ocean's depths, where life's spark ignited, universal laws prevailed, shaping existence's core.

10. Among these laws stood None, restricting All's immeasurable expanse. None sowed decay throughout creation, branding all that exists.

11. By None's decree, death became inevitable, and suffering an ever-present companion in living minds.

12. Confronting None's darkness, all things strove for survival, perpetuating cycles of birth, maturity, and demise.

13. Conscious creations, driven by meaning, engaged actively in their tasks, fulfilling cosmic roles.

14. Humanity, nature's pinnacle of comprehension, embodied the universe's subtle mechanisms. Yet men, though sagacious, stayed humble before those above them — the Guardians.

15. The Guardians devised and protected humanity's existence, forging essential laws and brokering alliances with the mysterious Lord of the Black. Thus, once-disputed statutes between light and darkness solidified into unchanging principles, now preserved by the Guardians.

16. Their adherence sprang from deep knowledge of cosmic order. Having ratified and accepted these laws, they carry out the Father's and Son's mission, sustaining cosmic equilibrium.

17. Though seemingly boundless, the Guardians too face certain creative confines.

18. They yearn for the day warfare with the Lords ends, so they might return to All's unity, where boundaries and separations vanish into an infinite oneness.

4.2.4

Adam and Eve's tale highlights conquering oneself, evolving, and the lasting impact of deeds. Parents' wisdom and the need to embrace fear and blaze a personal trail are vital amid human constraints. Themes of change, fortitude, and renewal underscore how nature and the human spirit can transcend adversity. A message of hope and empowerment reminds us of transformation's promise and creativity's role in shaping the universe.

1. We are earthborn beings, rooted on this planet with our own destiny.

2. Our paramount conquest is mastery of ourselves — overcoming fears, doubts, frailty. We must harness emotion, thought, and deed for true freedom.

3. Millennia of evolution shape us; we keep learning and broadening our grasp. Our potential reaches ever higher, birthing a prophesied one, surpassing all limitations.

4. Earthly faculties continually develop. We are not but creatures of the soil, bound intimately to our planet's core.

5. Some call themselves , a notion of decline and backwardness, denying our authentic essence and terrestrial ties.

6. Our ancestor Adam, arising from the Southern Sea, was born of parents inferior to him, yet he never dismissed the gifts they bestowed.

7. Nor could he erase their imprint, just as we cannot shed our heritage.

8. Adam mirrored his parents in form and being, though endowed with advanced knowledge, propelling him to learn from his makers and acknowledge life and death.

9. His consciousness was distinct, enabling him to confront creeping shadows. Yet Adam's path was not solitary.

10. Fate intertwined him with Eve — a radiant complement — united in profound oneness. Together, they seeded

society, trusting in shared sacrifice to thrive.

11. Their bond marked the primal, unwritten laws born not of external dictates but of their hearts. These laws sprang from their survival instincts amid a harsh world.

12. Yet they sought more than mere reaction; they longed to shape destiny. Guided by nature and the Guardians' ancient covenant, they established laws that resonated with their innermost truths.

13. Fear, that ancient bond, brought them together, fostering mutual burdens and a communal humanity. Rather than stifling them, fear became an impetus for love, pleasure, triumph, and the procreation of future generations.

14. From these acts arose the foundation of societies and governments. They built towers, tilled the fields, and, though they might declare, "See what my hands have built," they remained humbled in their self-awareness.

15. We must surpass our limited nature. Like the forests of men, we may stand tall, proclaiming our vigor. But genuine greatness transcends numbers or force. It rests in daring to face fears and forge an original path.

16. In nature, even towering trees sway in the gentlest breeze, branches quivering under the wind's touch. Nonetheless, they boast their might as mountains, unyielding despite the slightest gust.

17. So, too, in human society—kingdoms, tribes, temples—our established structures yield to the winds of change. Though we trust families and neighbors for stability, time's currents eventually alter our lives.

18. I, the wind, shall stir you and bring you under my influence. Like a gale moving mountains and rattling bedrock, I will shake temple and realm alike. Our constructs, shaped by hands, environment, and necessity, shall be shattered by my testimony.

19. Yet fear not, for I am also the wind bearing renewal. Where mountains have fallen to dust,

they shall resurrect, reaching the sky's loftiest heights.

20. When faced with adversity, I will lift you, unveiling the power latent within.

21. In striving for success, we perpetually evolve and adjust, but decay is unavoidable, marking all with time's imprint.

22. I come for a purpose beyond mortal reach — to raise, embolden, and restore mountains worn by nature and years.

23. In silent witness, these mountains reflect our flaws, rousing humility. Yet though men fail, my everlasting truths remain a steadfast anchor, guiding us to untapped potential.

24. Mountains have endured endless storms and eras, offering sage counsel to any who ask. Despite human frailty, I will raise them again, exemplifying nature's might and man's unyielding spirit.

25. A vicious assault shattered the family's very core, leaving desolation in its wake. This loss inflicted sorrow and hopelessness, severing the bonds that once united them.

26. Procreation is a sacred calling, granting every living being slow dominion over the cosmos. With each new child, we inherit ancestral wisdom and forge the future. The continuation of life ensures our species' survival and cosmic mission.

### 4.2.5

FAMILY, unity, resilience, power, and self-mastery are examined. The family's value, man and woman's sacred bond, child-rearing, and life's transitory nature appear. Striving for power, conquering oneself, and self-discovery feature strongly. Chosen trees symbolize resilience and capacity for change.

1. The First Eternal shines as a beacon of unity, leading every seeker along their way. In the trials of mortal life, the family is our ark of triumph and hope.

2. The father, a strong provider; the mother, a nurturing soul — together they sustain their children. Bound by mutual support, the family mirrors the universe's harmony.

3. Man and woman's sacred bond fortifies the family's stability. The woman tempers the man's ardor; in turn, the man yields his autonomy to fulfill her yearnings. Their union, weaving masculine and feminine energies, produces life's cradle.

4. Children enter the world entrusted to education in universal truth. Like seeds in fertile ground, they carry destiny's potential, equipped for the universe's challenges.

5. Our roots, shaped by ancient ways, anchor us to the earth's depths. Its bounty nurtures life in boundless generosity. From earth we rise and to earth we return.

6. At a mortal's final breath, may they find rest amid the crumbled mountains — a reminder of corporeal impermanence.

7. Though forests and mountains quake, their summits forever aspire skyward. Such is humanity's united spirit. Let forests thrive, and the mightiest trees stand firm.

8. From humble beginnings, our forebears traversed the earth, claiming it as their own. Their wanderlust ignites in us the ambition to carve fresh paths and embrace life's expanse.

9. In this changing realm, only the strong endure, while the weak vanish. Forest fires serve as crucibles, burning the frail, letting only the robust endure.

10. These resolute trees, thick-trunked and indomitable, reflect the unconquerable spirit vital for humanity's future. Just as they withstood the flames, we find strength in adversity.

11. The blaze of my words signifies the trials and hardships we face. Those who embrace these ordeals emerge tempered and unbreakable, forging real power that endures.

12. Yet authentic power transcends outward feats. It hinges on vanquishing the self. Have you faced your own

depths — acknowledged your fears — and bested your frailties? True might is honed within.

13. So, in life's inferno, emulate the forest's endurance. Welcome adversity, unleash might against evil, endure each trial. But never forget self-conquest, for genuine strength lies there.

14. The charge to conquer, rising up the ladder of mastery, emerges as guiding truth. Begin with self-rule, then expand to family, tribe, nation, people, world, cosmos, and beyond. Through conquest, the individual's, the collective's, and the universal's survival are secured.

15. Power equates to survival. Broader dominion fortifies preservation. Thus, ultimate virtue arises from acts that broaden survival's domain. The greatest conqueror stands as unmatched symbol of might, inspiring awe and deterring threats.

16. To conquer without hypocrisy is the hallmark of sincerity. Though war often is deemed malignant, its crucible can serve noble aims, forging individuals and civilizations in adversity's fires.

17. The highest virtue is None's overthrow: an act of creation and sustenance, defying the void's dominion. By partaking in this triumph, we celebrate our essence and contribute to the universe's grand mosaic.

18. Attuning to your inner compass, you fulfill destiny, each soul's unique place in creation. The journey entails discovering your true self, forging harmony with cosmic purpose.

19. As towering trees in adversity shelter the weak, so do a chosen few stand as bulwarks of strength. Receiving the sacred edict, they extend solace to those in despair, a sanctuary in life's storm.

20. Probing these venerable trees unravels the essence and pathway toward All. Through their teachings, one learns self-truth and grasps deeper purpose.

21. Mankind's roots tangle in the earth, flowing like lifeblood through the soul. The earth unites us, the stars beckon us.

22. Bound to the ground, we conquer from within, subjugating our interior frontiers — fears, doubts, illusions.

23. The chosen trees of my forests, unburned by my flames, shall endure and ascend, ruling every realm.

24. Temples will collapse yet be raised anew under our guardianship; kingdoms shall kneel, then rally behind our banner.

25. I, the Scribe, have secretive but capable warriors who soon shall emerge from shadow.

26. My voice will echo across the land, binding divided peoples once their fortresses lie fallen. Then, in that ruin, they shall embrace hope.

27. You are the green forests of men, your roots delving deep into life's soil.

28. There, in the mind's recesses, the key to eradicating None awaits — the seedbed of all creation in this realm.

## 4.3

### 4.3.1

SELF-LOVE, family, and love in general are emphasized. Love can transform lives and create a better world. Children and friendships are discussed. Victory comes from loving oneself and overcoming inner obstacles. The will of the Father of All can bring enlightenment and power. Your true nature and purpose may be found in defeating None, which represents the absence of all that is.

1. The first love is the love of your true self. It is the purest and most genuine form of love, for it does not hinge on external conditions or expectations.

2. By discovering your true self, you free yourself from illusions and attachments that hold you captive.

3. May our love be like a beam of light passing endlessly between two mirrors, traveling forever between their surfaces.

4. Our love reflects the light, radiating hope and inspiration, helping us overcome every challenge.

5. Before you can share love with others, you must first love yourself — accepting and valuing who you are, both strengths and frailties.

6. When you love yourself, you can give and receive love unreservedly, your heart open to boundless possibilities.

7. Seek love within and then offer it to others, passing it from one soul to another.

8. Love is a treasure that transforms lives and shapes the world for us and posterity.

9. A family is built on the love binding two people. Flowing between them like a current, it extends to their children.

10. The family is a sacred entity anchoring society. The love it embodies strengthens and preserves its members.

11. The love of a family nurtures the children born of it, conferring safety and guidance for their growth.

12. The kingdom is robust when families thrive, since children are its future and bearers of light.

13. Friendships arise from mutual love and respect, forging meaningful bonds that supply solace and fellowship.

14. May our realms mirror this light, contributing to the victory of all. Let us labor to forge a realm of esteem and harmony.

15. The path to triumph lies in loving oneself, extending that love outward until absolute victory is won.

16. Triumph is not seizing others but conquering internal barriers. Through loving ourselves and each other, anything is possible.

17. Uncover your essence as the light of the universe, delving into your being to find who you truly are. You are a spark of the , capable of creating whatever you envision.

18. The will that springs from the mouth of the Father of All enlightens the divided self to its authentic identity, for the Father's will is the fount of creation.

19. Power is the capacity to endure, the currency of achievement, nurtured by tapping the Father's will.

20. Good fosters communion with All, sustaining life; evil severs and kills. Good and evil are judged relative to the Father's will.

21. Seek your genuine nature, individually and collectively, unveiling your destiny in conquering None, the void of all that is. Extend your being's power, commanding all beyond yourself.

### 4.3.2

Embrace the Scribe and self-discovery to unlock possibilities. Break free from those stifling truth. Our inner light can remain hidden, but discarding illusions unleashes our radiance. Interconnectedness yields beauty and meaning. Respect the rights of others and chase your dreams. Helping others clarifies our own goals. We reap the energy we sow. Our actions echo our feelings, so offering positivity and kindness ensures the same in return.

1. Accept my words, and every path shall open for you. Defy those who reject truth, journey inward, and discover your ultimate fate.

2. Overcome those who would suppress truth and embark upon self-discovery to unearth your destiny.

3. Our inner light can be obscured by darkness, like a mirror hidden from sight. Stripping away that veil frees us from illusions and constraints.

4. Radiate until your brilliance pierces the night, lighting your route and dissolving all frontiers.

5. You and I are mirrors of one another, reflections of our interconnected being. Through this recognition, we forge remarkable beauty and purpose.

6. We are all nodes of All, inseparable links within a grand design, each seeking reunion with our True Self—a state of unbounded love and rapture.

7. Every node possesses a personal legend awaiting revelation through the unfolding of will. This right merits universal respect.

8. Our liberty to follow and fulfill our dreams is bounded by our obligation to uphold that same liberty for others.

9. Only by esteeming others' aspirations do we gain clearer insight into our own.

10. To act against another and inflict harm is to harm oneself, for all is connected. Hence, tending to others with kindness and respect serves our highest good.

11. By blessing others, we receive blessings in return, for the universe reciprocates the energy we project.

12. Our deeds reflect who we are and how we treat others. We are all mirrors, so kindness offered is kindness regained.

13. Pursuing dreams while honoring others' freedom ensures a smoother journey, free of needless tension. Blocking another's progress shackles our own.

14. Whatever light we radiate returns upon us. Offer positivity and grace, and the universe responds in kind.

### 4.3.3

PRINCIPLES FOR a life of fulfillment: self-love, acceptance of shared bonds, and alignment with cosmic truth. Governments should attain peace through mutual respect and cooperation. Spreading these principles is a shared duty for a brighter tomorrow. Freedom must intertwine with justice. Believers aim to foster good worldwide.

1. My responsibility is to seek my legend, a singular and purposeful road, while honoring others' roads in turn.

2. Those who strive for destiny shall root their actions in self-love and the awareness of universal connectedness.

3. My words offer sanctuary and light in the world's darkest reaches.

4. Embracing my precepts yields enlightenment and reveals one's true calling.

5. Each path upholds its boundaries, balancing freedom with duty.

6. My principles, grounded in the earth, were entrusted by the Guardians to earnest seekers of depth.

7. Previously, rulers coveted peace as the final aim, yet used violence and oppression to claim it. Through enlightenment, peace may arise from empathy and joint effort.

8. Therefore, any who yearn for destiny must diffuse these principles and illuminate governments worldwide.

9. Those governments shall guarantee each person's freedom, revoking it only for perpetrators of grave injustice.

10. People who reject others' journeys and commit crimes lose their rightful path and may be fairly penalized.

11. Adherents of these principles shall scatter their light, realizing it across all realms. Adopting these principles becomes a source of enlightenment, compelling them to share its wisdom and compassion, bettering our future.

4.3.4

STRIVE FOR achievement without harming anyone. Cultivate inner might, harmonize with the will of All, and respect each life's journey. Do not intrude on others' paths; engage in upright conduct. Creation and destruction interlace in cosmic balance, preserved by survival and elimination. Love is championed as the conquering power. Align your will with All and pursue collective triumph and prosperity, never harming a single soul.

1. We aim to weave success without wounding others. To reach this height, we fortify ourselves

inwardly, shaping the world in line with our will.

2. Such devotion demands unwavering concentration, for solely by harmonizing with All's will can we overcome and prevail.

3. The will of All, embodying flawless potential, operates through each soul's distinct passage. Each being's path advances its inherent purpose. Unity with All arises from alignment with its will, enabling communal triumph while preserving individuality.

4. We must embrace our own path and honor others' freedom. Every person's journey is sacred and never contradicts or suppresses another's. United, we forge links that yield prosperity, culminating in All's victory.

5. Interfering with another's way is grave wrongdoing, thwarting them from fulfilling destiny. Others reflect fragments of our divided self; we decide whether to merge or diverge. We must enlighten others through their consent, not contending with the uninformed, but traveling onward, unencumbered.

6. All righteous acts promoting survival accord with the Will of All, while destructive deeds lead to severance. Sabotaging another's path breeds ruin and fragmentation, the root of evil. Yet even darkest deeds may hold a glimmer of good, and seemingly noble acts can seed disaster.

7. Let us regard everyone as equal collaborators in reality, each seeking universal ends and personal quests. Uphold their choice of the righteous road, adding to the collective's survival.

8. The paradox of life is that creation and annihilation often coincide. What appears to destroy may serve life, and what ostensibly saves may doom us all.

9. Strength and downfall unfold through the survival of the fittest and elimination of the wicked, guided by ancient compacts. Fallen nations give way to those unyielding, who surmount all, starting with themselves.

10. Conquest is driven by love, yearning to merge with All, upholding individuality.

11. In death, those who embrace All's will flourish and ascend to unity's gate. Those resisting All's will vanish, plummeting into the void. The victory of All resides in unwavering pursuit of righteousness and freedom from evil.

12. In this cosmic tapestry, we serve as threads weaving an interwoven masterpiece. Let us align our wills with All's will, discovering self-knowledge and shared triumph.

13. Together we unravel the universe's mysteries, conquering each test, and shaping a realm of prosperity for every soul, harming none.

## 4.4

### 4.4.1

THE SCRIBE DESCRIBES the luminous potential within everyone. By aligning with rational self-interest and embracing our true selves, we can unlock our fullest capabilities. Self-realization leads to a harmonious life attuned to the cosmos. The Scribe underscores the importance of following All's will and uncovering our unique legend.

1. The end dwells within you. In the depths of heart and mind, you find your extraordinary potential and the path to a purposeful life.

2. Scattered across cosmic space, solitary stars blaze as proof of the energy within them. Their brilliance emerges not from outside but their hearts.

3. Although the space between stars appears empty, it brims with delicate, ethereal radiance that lights the void and connects celestial bodies, the stage for cosmic performance.

4. The elements forming the universe, including ourselves, arose in the stars' depths, where unrelenting fusion granted them a shared essence.

5. Each of us carries an inward spark, akin to night's shining stars. We are radiant beings, shining All's luminous presence.

6. All pervades all existence, yet binds none. All's infinite scope transcends limitation, forging a limitless field of promise.

7. By allowing All's light to shine through us, we transcend our divided selves and find the true end residing within. This transformation aligns with All's will.

8. As self-aware beings, we wage cosmic warfare against the emptiness of Nothingness. Our mission is to build and uphold our Legend, defying oblivion's yawning chasm.

9. We achieve this by following the Father's will, the ultimate wellspring of counsel and purpose. By yielding to this rational self-interest, we gain clarity and direction.

10. When we submit to All's will, a deep power awakens. Like the constellations above, we shine with hope and encourage others.

11. A massive, slumbering power lies hidden in your soul, awaiting your command. Awaken that titan and witness a wealth of talent beyond measure. Embrace that inner might, leading you to greatness.

12. Each person holds a reservoir of capacity, a limitless well of insight and vigor. Without tapping it, we drift in confusion, half alive. Recognize your deep well of potential, harness it, and shape a life rich in purpose.

13. Your birthright is extraordinary — to gleam as a star in the sky, imparting brilliance upon the earth. As you travel life's path, intensify this glow, guiding others and carving a place in history.

14. Within the cosmos's immensity, stars stand as steadfast sources of wonder. Let their unwavering glow remind you of your inner fortitude. Delve into your boundless power and wield it in all pursuits. Emulate the stars, steadfast and marvelous, leading the way in the darkness.

15. Aim to harmonize with the will of All, the cosmic current coursing through life. Doing so ensures your survival while furthering all living beings' progress. Failing to align invites stagnation here and beyond.

16. Just as stars adhere to their set orbits, we must accept the journey intended for us. The laws undergirding everything bind us, permitting no evasion. True growth emerges from surrender, revealing the wonder and purpose in existence.

17. Stars follow the same unyielding laws shaping our lives. They cannot flee their designated orbits or alter their fates. We likewise must accept our trials and constraints, for they carve our identity. By welcoming them bravely, we nurture resilience and wisdom.

18. As stars obey cosmic imperatives, they evolve and burn, fulfilling their roles. We likewise must embrace our responsibilities, living each day with devotion. By recognizing our place in the cosmic mosaic, we leave an enduring impact.

19. Let your inner luminescence blaze, even amid life's darkest corners, banishing ignorance and terror. By faithfully pursuing your destined course, you triumph over shadows, ushering in a world of hope and deepened insight.

20. True success springs from tuning yourself to the stars' cosmic paths and yielding to All's will. Embracing your innate force and resonating with universal law unseals a fulfilling life. Let the stars guide you, and All's will be your compass on life's journey.

21. Like a star's life must cease, your story's finale is fixed in the cosmic script. Accept this truth serenely, knowing that all must end. As your twilight nears, let your light intensify, leaving a heritage of compassion and wisdom.

22. A star's light cannot be concealed. So, too, the splendor of your soul will shine for all to see. Your distinct radiance will scatter across the world in its glow.

23. Truth and illumination abound, yet our limits often obscure them. To truly perceive and discard our ignorance, we must coordinate our will with the collective will of All.

24. By rejecting fragmentation and embracing harmony, we move into self-realization, unleashing our hidden greatness. A moment of profound shift is

imminent, unveiling knowledge of our authentic self, intensifying until we gleam like starlight overhead.

25. As darkness recedes, success unfolds via survival and the lasting legacy of what we shape in this world.

### 4.4.2

THE SCRIBE URGES each soul to radiate inner light, surmount limits, and enhance the world. His message: realize your inner might, live in tune with cosmic order, and aspire to a worthy, fulfilling life.

1. The Halls of the Dead await, prepared to honor us based on our acceptance and fulfillment of our singular legends. Each mortal walks a chosen course, guided by personal standards.

2. None can ordain our fate; as descendants of the Father and wards of the Guardians, we hold the sacred right to define our future.

3. Though paradoxes might obscure our understanding, unveiling the truth of ourselves expands wisdom and radiance.

4. Like heavenly bodies, we beam across creation, inevitably expressing the truths held within. The chosen cannot hide their core essence, which cuts through darkness and topples obstacles.

5. Once ignited, their flame intensifies until the end. As humble fragments of a higher Self, we strive to surpass limitations by grasping existence's true essence.

6. Victory dwells in our will, conjoined to All's will, anchored by the knowledge of our legend, awakened by this sacred union.

7. I am one who has merged with All and now reflects flawless light for humankind.

8. They who have crossed the Gateway offer light from beyond, a sacrifice for the people.

9. Its reflection remains imperfect — channeled through flawed

lenses — and their sacrifice is their toil upon the Way.

10. As stars grow in brilliance when approached, so truth multiplies truth.

11. I am a star, bearing witness to the light for all. Emulate me, sharing the light I have bestowed.

12. I am the world's light, empowering all to shine like heaven's stars. The brilliance of my stars conveys truth, rooted in the will of All, which steers the cosmic laws.

13. That starlight does not come from outside but from All manifesting in every being, linking all and revealing the universe's unity.

14. My light springs from within me, reflecting the oneness of my will with All. This alignment grants creation's power, manifesting my aspirations for the greater good.

15. The will of All stands as the ladder we climb to attain freedom and widen our might. Tethering our will to All's, we adopt a rational self-interest, becoming agents of beneficence on earth.

16. Our wills must never depart from All's will, vital to sustaining balance and peace of mind. Conflicting with universal will arouses distress and detaches us from our essence.

17. The stars' might emerges from the will of All shaped by the laws of this universe — celestial bodies that embody creation and metamorphosis, hinting at humanity's unlimited capacity.

18. Our power surges from the same rift as the stars, enabling us to rule all. We share the cosmos's creative might, though guided by empathy and love.

19. From instinct through reason to awareness, we strive to master the universe ever more skillfully. All of life is the creative property of will, bounded by None.

20. Like stars, we brighten the cosmos, refining ourselves from within, a near-ultimate mission. By cultivating self-knowledge, compassion, and insight, we elevate existence.

21. We hold all we need to defeat None. These resources lie in each corner of our world and within

our souls, waiting for us to tap them.

22. The Father's will, the Son's light, the Mother's love cleave the darkness, set firmly in our hands. Such unity of will, logic, and love conquers the night.

23. Authentic faith and grasp, matured through growth, can liberate the soul and awaken its cosmic bond, turning us from falsehood and harmful mindsets.

24. The eight has been conferred on us as a catalyst for success. Adopting its spirit, we harness the earth's abundance, forging a link with the Eternals of All, unveiling wisdom and enlightenment.

25. The eight paves the way to fathoming life's riddles, discovering our place in creation, and realizing our singular destiny.

26. By heeding the eight, we forge a deeper bond with the universal Will, transcending our own egos to embrace a grander vision, fostering empathy and comprehension.

27. I, who have tasted truth and journeyed through the Gateway with the Guardians' counsel, carry to you the illuminating fire of knowledge.

28. Behold my scars, testaments to the price I paid for your good. Let the light of understanding I bring transform you into luminaries of insight.

29. Only light guards our passing.

# 8

## 8.1

TO BECOME a Zion citizen, aspirants must seek the sacred city, embrace the law, and enter a solemn Contract and Covenant. This marks their devotion to self-mastery and transformation, including conquering the dragon within. At nineteen, aspirants formally join the citizenry by accepting the Scribe's law, emphasizing sincerity, truth, and submission. Citizens uphold the law, cultivate justice, and bolster Zion's progress, attaining growth, fulfillment, and opportunities for uplifting the world.

1. To earn Zion citizenship, one embarks on a deep quest of self-discovery and commitment.

2. The journey begins by seeking the holy city of Zion, aided by the wisdom of the Seven or guidance from a member of the XIX.

3. Upon arrival, the aspirant must embrace the Guardians' law — principles by which Zion is governed.

4. They then enter a solemn Contract and Covenant, swearing fealty to the Scribe's law and pledging unwavering obedience for life.

5. This Contract and Covenant is no mere rite but a deeply personal vow, revealing one's dedication to pursuing both legend and the Will of All.

6. The aspirant must confront the dragon within, symbolizing inner demons and obstacles to personal growth — a trial demanding bravery, diligence, and relentless self-betterment.

7. At the age of nineteen, the aspirant may officially become a Zion citizen by accepting the Scribe's law and joining Zion's civil domain.

8. One must fully grasp the Contract's meaning—its negation and affirmation—and be certain, free from doubts or uncertainties.

9. Honesty and sincerity are paramount in Zion. Any malicious intent, falsehood, or deceit stands forbidden.

10. Submitting wholeheartedly to the Scribe's just requirements is vital; tasks are performed with utmost earnestness, seeking only the Guardians' favor—acceptance sharply diverging from rejection.

11. Every citizen's Contract and Covenant is recorded in writing and guarded by the city, with an official copy preserved in the XIX's secure vaults.

12. Furthermore, the city must publicly sanction one's Contract and Covenant by a sustaining vote of all present, affirming membership in Zion's fellowship.

13. Becoming a citizen places one within a collective striving for humanity's betterment. Citizens safeguard the Scribe's law, champion equity and goodwill, and contribute to Zion's advancement.

14. Though demanding, the path to citizenship yields deep personal growth, fulfillment, and the power to shape the world for good.

## 8.2

THE GATEWAY brings transformation to the chosen. Once veiled, now restored, it guides those prepared to evolve. Self-perfection is key for entering. Preparation spans varied dimensions. The Gateway's secrets are reserved for masters, but some are shared for readiness. Seekers must persevere, led by grace and tenacity.

1. The Guardians grant certain chosen ones the Gateway—an immeasurable treasure—and a transformative path commences.

2. Having released hidden truths from humankind, the Guardians entrusted Adam and his heirs in Eden with secreting the orb away from covetous hands.

3. Through the line of judges, from Abraham to Levi, the orb remained safe until Dan's betrayal shattered it.

4. The Gateway has reappeared, bearing a chosen spirit. At the destined hour, this soul shall undergo profound change through its power.

5. Gaining entry demands a course of self-perfection. The Sixteen, Eight, Four, Two, and One — holy principles — guide the pilgrim toward enlightenment.

6. Intention, location, age, and other elements shape the preparation for this weighty undertaking.

7. Before performing the second practice of the Eight and entering the Gateway, the seeker must resolve to do so. With unwavering focus, they train mind and body, forging a link to the Will of All. They select a site, kept secret from the unworthy.

8. A pristine, undefiled area is prepared, yet if trapped among adversaries, one may choose prudently.

9. Age is crucial: those over eleven partake to fortify themselves, while those past seventy are exempt. The ill, traveling, or expectant can delay their cycles until circumstances permit.

10. Keeping in touch with one's Will of All is vital; time is set aside thrice daily — morn, noon, and dusk — to face west and commune with the Seven Mountains' Guardians. For men, women, and hermits alike, the West remains the compass of will.

11. Ritual purity precedes each cycle: hands and faces washed in cold water, invigorating mind and body alike.

12. Two cycles exist: the lesser cycle (twice daily) and the greater cycle (once). The lesser cycle involves reciting portions of the One and recalling the Guardians who gave us being, invoking them by the Father's name.

13. The greater cycle, a deeper rite, entails ablutions, finding a fitting

place, and sitting westward. After declaring intention, one focuses every thought into the present, acknowledging All's boundless wisdom.

14. The Gateway's depths remain reserved for the chosen masterful few. Yet a portion of its mysteries is entrusted to earthly folk, paving the way for mightier revelations.

15. Seekers are urged to persist, for when readiness and worthiness fuse, the Gateway unveils itself.

16. The Guardians' grace and the individual's devotion will guide them along this sacred path.

## 8.3

Every first day of the week, Zion's citizens assemble to revere the Scribe and the Guardians. Seven chosen sages guide them. Citizens fulfill tasks set by the XIX.

1. On the first day of each week, Zion's populace unites in homage to the Scribe and the Guardians — a solemn moment to reflect on their might and wisdom.

2. Zion's citizenry is led by the Seven, individuals distinguished by insight, virtue, and deep roots in the city's guiding tenets.

3. Should the Seven be absent or unable, a temporary group of seven shall stand in their place, preserving Zion's direction and stability.

4. As the citizens gather, they undertake prescribed duties in accordance with the XIX's commands — whether prayerful devotions, contemplations, or acts of service.

5. By honoring these duties, Zion's people strengthen communal ties and further the city's progress, living as one under the Scribe's guiding star.

## 8.4

CITIZENS CONTRIBUTE five percent of their income to support the city, which in turn sends ten percent of its total to the capital. Transparent governance is upheld via an annual public ledger.

1. Each citizen dedicates five percent of their earnings to the city's treasury — an affirmation of loyalty and unity.

2. In return, five percent of the city's full revenue is remitted to the capital, bolstering shared bonds and ensuring synergy in Zion.

3. A detailed annual record is carefully compiled, disclosing how collected tithes are spent.

4. This open report reaffirms prudent stewardship, showing citizens how their contributions foster the city's well-being.

## 8.5

A HALLOWED calendar marks high days and low days for solemn observation, forging milestones in citizens' lives and enriching their communal spirit.

1. A sacred timeline designates significant days observed with utmost reverence by Zion's citizens and the XIX. High days hold profound weight.

2. The Day of the Birth of the Scribe commemorates his arrival, whose teachings form Zion's bedrock. Citizens gather to honor his legacy.

3. The Day of the Sending of the Twelve and Revelation of the Scribe's Book recalls the moment the twelve disciples spread his wisdom. It's a day of celebration, lauding their sacrifices.

4. The Day of the Battle of Armageddon stands as a solemn remembrance of the grand clash between light and shadow. It calls

for unity, courage, and upholding Zion's ideals.

5. The Day of the Departure of the Tribes marks when Zion's twelve tribes ventured to other worlds, bearing the Scribe's counsel and the mandate of strength and justice — both sorrowful and hopeful.

6. Between Zion's high days lie the low days:

7. The Day of the Entry into the Gateway honors the Scribe's passage into the celestial orb, a time for reflection on the gifts bestowed upon Zion.

8. The Day of the Gathering of the Army of the Scribe pays tribute to the band of warriors committed to defending his principles, pledging loyalty and devotion.

9. The Day of the Relighting of the Temple Fire symbolizes renewal under adversity, as the sacred flame in Zion's Temple is reignited.

10. The Day of the Exile of the Scribe observes a moment of thanksgiving when the tribes depart, and the Scribe journeys alone, leaving citizens to contemplate his abiding lessons.

11. All citizens perform their duties on these revered days, adhering to directives from the XIX. Through such observances, Zion's people honor their past, celebrate the present, and aspire to a brighter destiny.

## 8.6

CITIZENS UNDERTAKE a nineteen-day pilgrimage of fasting, reflection, and preparing a dedicated space for introspection. Fasting purifies and sharpens awareness, while self-inquiry reveals deeper purpose. Upon completing this vigil, citizens emerge rejuvenated, emboldened as warriors of light with renewed resolve and gratitude.

1. At least once in a lifetime, a citizen is summoned to a transformative nineteen-day

pilgrimage, marked by fasting, introspection, and sacred travel.

2. At the journey's outset, they consecrate a sanctuary — perhaps a secluded retreat or a private chamber — where silence and self-examination can flourish.

3. For nineteen days, they practice abstinence, purging body and spirit, allowing clarity of thought and heightened perception.

4. Reflection forms the pilgrimage's core: a delving into thoughts, emotions, and intentions. In so doing, they unearth their essence and life's mission.

5. Throughout this vigil, citizens keep their mind on their legend and the Will of All. The legend is each one's unique narrative; the Will of All, the plan guiding creation.

6. Synchronizing with their legend and the Will of All, they attain a profound sense of purpose, transcending ego's confines and channeling universal wisdom.

7. Concluding the nineteen days, they emerge as enlightened warriors, carrying renewed conviction, deeper self-knowledge, and reverence for life's sacredness.

## 8.7

AT NINETEEN years of age or beyond, citizens may join the XIX. After a careful review, those deemed worthy undergo a quest, proving their readiness. Upon induction, they become sentinels, pledged to protect citizens and serve in high regard.

1. Any citizen nineteen or older wishing to serve in the XIX may begin by contacting a member or submitting a written appeal. No station is barred, provided they fulfill prerequisites.

2. These include a clean record — no grave offenses — settled tax obligations, and at least nineteen months' city citizenship before eligibility.

3. The XIX conducts an extensive assessment. Should the candidate pass, they confront a final trial, a quest confirming their fitness.

4. Completion signals acceptance as a full-fledged XIX member, leaving their city to join the sentinels safeguarding Zion's inhabitants.

5. Once sworn in, they bear responsibility for ensuring every citizen's peace. The XIX's membership ranks among Zion's most honored, instilling trust and confidence throughout the land.

### 8.8

UPON DEATH, citizens must donate nineteen percent of their estate to the XIX, ensuring Zion's welfare, after settling debts and prioritizing minor children's needs.

1. When a citizen passes, they are entrusted to the Guard in the Halls of the Dead. From their possessions, nineteen percent is rendered to the XIX's upkeep.

2. Nonetheless, any unsettled debts and obligations must first be discharged.

3. The welfare of minor children takes precedence, ensuring their security before offering resources to the XIX.

4. Thus the ordered process is maintained — settling responsibilities, then dedicating a portion to sustaining Zion through the XIX.

# 16

## 16.1

THE SCRIBE FINDS himself in another world. He sees three red suns, golden stars, and azure grass swaying. In the center, a tremendous obsidian cube revolves, and a voice summons him.

1. I stand upon a planet unknown to me, grander than the one I call home. A realm of alien splendor stretches before my eyes, stirring awe in my heart.

2. Overhead, three blazing red suns cast their fiery glow across a sky of brilliant orange. Yet golden stars still shine on high, testifying to the union of heaven and earth.

3. Underfoot, a vast expanse of azure grass bends in a warm breeze that soothes my soul, and an orchestra of sound emerges, the wind's whispers harmonizing with the gentle rustle of leaves.

4. Above, colossal clouds drift across a silver sky like galleons at sea, throwing long shadows on the land. Their shifting shapes remind me of the universe's endless potential.

5. At the heart of this field, an immense obsidian cube slowly spins. Its sleek, reflective faces gleam in the light, sending faint reflections across its surroundings.

6. A voice, mightier than thunder, calls out: "Come!"

7. Falling to my knees, I fervently pray. My spirit quivers with anticipation for the purpose that beckons me. Nearing the threshold of the sanctuary's secrets, I shall face the Guardians and absorb the wisdom of All.

## 16.2

There is a link between stability and change. The cosmos perpetually evolves, while stagnation leads to irrelevance. This vision ignites the desire to pursue deeper understanding.

1. A revelation unfolds: the universe's workings and nature's patterns glow before me.

2. Gazing at the base of the obsidian cube, I witness it shifting in all directions, yet it keeps a stable core, unmoved.

3. From this insight, I learn that nature's steadfastness intertwines with its ceaseless metamorphosis, and we, in turn, seek stability through that very change.

4. At a perplexing crossroads, we stand, reconciling this paradox with vigilant awareness.

5. Across its boundlessness, the universe is forever in motion; nothing remains fixed.

6. Stagnation—absence of change—breeds irrelevance and ultimate decay.

7. Deep within, I sense this vision offers but a fragment of a grander design, urging me to chase knowledge unrelentingly.

8. Thus, I see that change, in all guises, emerges as the single constant within the cosmic vastness.

## 16.3

Receiving a second vision, the Scribe roams a realm of marvels, spurring a cosmic thirst for knowledge. Through study and exploration, the universe's unity is revealed, inspiring reverence for its intricate beauty. Uniting with fellow seekers, the Scribe embarks on a shared quest, unveiling creation's mysteries.

1. A fresh vision dawns, transporting me beyond my boldest dreams. Vibrant hues and enthralling shapes form a panorama like no other.

2. I traverse this celestial realm in reverent wonder, encountering colossal wheels of fire blazing in the heavens, their radiance lighting the entire domain.

3. In the midst of this astral display, I perceive the presence of emptiness — yet it is not a void but an infinite potential from which all creation springs. Awe overwhelms me as I grasp that this nothingness fuels all possibility.

4. Driven by longing for the universe's hidden truths, I realize diligent study and comprehension of all things hold the key. Immersing myself in nature's tapestry will reveal cosmic patterns that form a mighty fortress against any threat.

5. Overcoming obstacles, I persist, seeking to master nature's magnitude. Each revelation intensifies my motivation and yearning for knowledge.

6. Gradually, reality's concealed layers open to me, an endless puzzle of interconnected parts. Subatomic realms to spiraling galaxies link in cosmic harmony, each part rippling through the whole.

7. My deepening insight stirs veneration and humility, unveiling the cosmos's delicate equilibrium. The universe's beauty humbles me, underscoring how much still awaits discovery.

8. In time, I recognize the laws of nature as fluid and dynamic, reflecting a universe in perpetual flux. My curiosity soars higher, compelling me to venture past every limit of understanding.

9. As my castle of knowledge grows, I meet other earnest seekers, forging a haven of shared wisdom. We merge our insights and glean still more profound truths.

10. In that collaborative pursuit, veils lift, revealing subtler aspects of reality. Together, we stretch beyond narrow perceptions to hear the cosmos whisper its secrets.

11. A life-altering passage transpires, etched forever in my spirit. After calling upon a sacred sanctuary, I'm gifted this second vision — a glimpse of cosmic majesty, sparking unquenchable curiosity.

12. Devoted to uncovering the nature of All, I fortify my inner

stronghold of understanding. Deeper ties to the world expose its splendid complexity and abiding unity.

## 16.4

THE SCRIBE marvels at the cosmos's splendor. The Guardians bring solace, and the First Eternal extends comfort. Reverence and gratitude fill the Scribe's heart as the universe's harmony and precision stir awe. Creation's countless forms reveal its perfection.

1. A new vision arises, blanketing my mind with majesty and wonder. Around me, the universe's vastness envelops me like a warm mantle.

2. Within this grand tableau, the Guardians stand as vigilant stewards, stirring confidence in their watchful presence. My thoughts linger on the First Eternal, source of creation's love and mercy, infusing me with a sense of purpose.

3. A kaleidoscope of emotions surges — wonder, humility, gratitude — revealing how enigmatically beautiful existence is. The bond uniting all life resonates deep within my soul.

4. From humble microbes to colossal galaxies, each realm brims with carefully wrought order. This cosmic dance of symmetry exalts an incomparable cosmic intelligence.

5. Living creatures, in their infinite variety, parade before my mind as reflections of creation's artistry. From a bird's flamboyant plumage to a butterfly's fragile wings, from an agile gazelle's grace to a newborn's gentle gaze, the extravagance of life captivates me.

6. I ponder man's form, shaped by the Guardians' wisdom, granted free will by the First Eternal. Man stands as a master and a soldier of All, capable of immeasurable love, compassion, and transformation.

## 16.5

Guided by a Guardian emissary, the Scribe undergoes trials and strict purification across nineteen days to prove worthy of the sought powers. The emissary, a radiant being of cosmic majesty, unveils its true form and grants crowns. As the obsidian cube's rotation halts and a dark doorway emerges, the Scribe feels drawn to confront the next phase of his quest.

1. Driven by fierce purpose, I advance toward the towering cube — silent walls rising like sentinels of ancient secrets.

2. I stand resolute at their base, proclaiming, "I have come far and shall return as often as needed, for it is my will to uncover the sanctuary's depths and unravel its mysteries."

3. From the cube's recesses echoes a voice: "Observe our emissary, your true ally. Prepare for trials of mastery — tests that will shape you into a vessel fit for the truths you crave."

4. A figure descends from the Second Eternal, radiant in shimmering light. The emissary, an embodiment of celestial grace, appears before me, an illuminating torch amid my mortal weakness.

5. With a voice resonant as time, the emissary asks, "Who are you, seeking mastery of the sealed mystery?"

6. "I am the Scribe," I answer, unflinching, "chosen by the Guardians to confront and defeat King None."

7. "Very well," the emissary replies. "But say — do you hold the Word, that sacred utterance granting you the power you seek?"

8. My humility stirs me to confess, "No, but the Guardians hold it for me, a treasure I am not yet worthy to claim."

9. Wordless, the emissary departs. An hour later, he returns in reverent awe: "The Guardians have granted me the key that grants you sanctuary's entry," he whispers.

10. "But beware — the road ahead is steep. You must renounce worldly ease, adopting strict discipline. I shall guide you, but success rests upon you alone."

11. Discontent led you here, yearning for more than a dull life left behind. Now, at the edge of the unknown, you heed the Guardians' distant murmur, summoning you on.

12. I urge you to wait in reflection, cleansing all frailties hindering your path. Only thus will you be free to embrace your will.

13. I insist you vow firm obedience, not blindly but with disciplined focus, unifying your drives in pursuit of your will. This vow unlocks your potential and forms your legend.

14. Every dimension of your being must be purified, from thought to deed, forging you anew to claim your grand task.

15. "In nineteen days, I shall return and manifest to you — provided you are worthy," the emissary says. A hush falls as the immense challenge dawns, but determination steels your heart.

16. For nineteen days, you strive for purity, discarding internal weights obstructing your Legend. Through meditation, reflection, mindful living, and physical training for war, you sharpen your mind and spirit.

17. On the nineteenth day, a radiant light advances, until it takes a luminous shape before you.

18. "You have proved worthy of the mysteries," proclaims the emissary. "You are cleansed of burdens thwarting your Legend."

19. "I shall reveal myself so you may see my essence and be transformed," the emissary continues. A wave of humility and gratitude floods you.

20. "For I am your servant, unveiling these mysteries of mysteries, and I shall crown you."

21. "No man comprehends his own Word nor that of another, nor the key to this secret," the emissary's words leave you pondering your inner wisdom.

22. The emissary's radiant cloak dissolves, unveiling a being robed in shimmering flames. In his hand rests a mace of crimson lightning;

his golden face bears fierce beauty; eyes of piercing blue. His hair of white fire undulates as if alive.

23. A force saturates your mind, forging a profound bond between you. Boundaries vanish, your souls uniting in an indescribable communion.

24. Euphoria surges, enveloping you in triumph's ecstasy and the fiery thrill of combat. The warrior within awakens, aflame with purpose.

25. A clarion sense of mission arises, urging you to fulfill your Legend, a destiny no longer distant but urgently present.

26. Suddenly, the rotating cube stills, and at its base, a darkened doorway materializes — a silent, beckoning threshold.

27. Drawn toward this enigmatic portal, you prepare for the next chapter of your journey, poised to face whatever mysteries lurk beyond.

## 16.6

IN A QUEST to explore deeper mysteries, the Scribe receives instructions from an emissary: craft an earthen image of the Father of All, reconcile inner light with darkness, and seek the limitless expanse of existence. The emissary promises to return on the nineteenth day.

1. The emissary's voice resonates with ancient authority: "Do you wish to pursue greater mysteries, the mystery of mysteries, if the path lies open before you?"

2. I answer, "I am willing, for it is my legend."

3. "Very well," the emissary replies. "Remain here and shape an earthen image of the Father of All. Bring unity to the light and darkness within you. Do not see me as a higher self. Instead, seek All, the vastness that surpasses all bounds. In this pursuit lies the core of your journey.

4. "Wait here, conquer your fears and restraints, and attend to my words upon my return."

5. With these instructions, the emissary departs, leaving me alone on the expanse of that

strange plain. As the days merge into nights, I abide in patience, wresting free from apprehension and inhibition, heeding the emissary's echoing counsel.

6. On the nineteenth day, the emissary does indeed appear before me.

## 16.7

AN EMISSARY challenges the Scribe to gain the strength to traverse the Void and honor the Guardians beyond existence. The Scribe commits wholeheartedly, discovering that real power stems from embracing love. Nineteen days later, the emissary proclaims the Scribe worthy and shows him a portal with a hidden staircase.

1. The emissary draws near again, addressing me in a voice older than time: "Have you gained the power to cross the unbounded Void and pay tribute to the Guardians who dwell beyond the edge of being?"

2. My spirit soars as I respond, "I have devoted myself entirely. I accept every challenge or sacrifice awaiting me. My resolve stands unshaken, and I shall not waver in this sacred quest."

3. The emissary's form glows with an otherworldly brilliance that transcends mortal confines. "Your devotion is praiseworthy, pilgrim of the Void. But understand: true might comes not solely from strength or learning. Only when you embrace All's love do you surpass yourself and commune with the cosmos."

4. As the emissary's words wash over me, I grasp an epiphany: love is that ineffable force binding creation. To traverse the Void and honor the Guardians, I must nurture love within. Like an arrow waiting on a bowstring, I must prime myself with intent and connection that outstrip any limit of the ego.

5. The emissary instructs me to behold all beings as a reflection of myself. If I prove worthy, he will

return in nineteen days. For those nineteen days, I strive to manifest love and shape the unity needed for ultimate surrender.

6. On the nineteenth day, the emissary reappears and declares me worthy—lover of all. He urges me to ignite remembrance of the Guardians and entreat them for freedom.

7. Following his counsel, I witness the veil draping the portal at the cube's base torn aside, unveiling a staircase beyond.

## 16.8

THE SCRIBE and the emissary tumble into a dark abyss, facing illusions devised to mislead the Scribe. With the emissary's help, he resists these falsehoods. A radiant woman halts his fall, guiding him into renunciation and renewal, signaling his rebirth and the dawn of a new state of being.

1. Approaching the door, the ground abruptly gives way, opening wide like a famished creature, swallowing us into its murky depths.

2. We plummet deeper into darkness, I clinging to the emissary's scarlet lightning mace. A faint gleam beckons overhead, a distant beacon in the endless void.

3. Illusions flit past, alluring phantoms meant to derail me. Yet I perceive them for the destructive lies they are, fending them off.

4. One illusion confronts me, asserting, "I am the shaper of forms, root of all things. All being flows from me." It promises dominion and might, tempting me to yield.

5. But the emissary stands firm, banishing the deceit with stern command.

6. "You have risen beyond humanity's confines," he proclaims, "but this is not your final station, lover of All. You are meant for loftier realms."

7. With those words, he withdraws his mace, letting me plunge further into the unseen blackness.

8. My fall is arrested by the arms of a radiant woman crowned in the sun's gold. The moon glimmers under her feet, and upon her brow shines a diadem of twelve stars.

9. At her side, I see a chalice of ornate silver and a dagger with a bone hilt.

10. Gently, I claim the dagger, slicing my palm so blood flows into the chalice. In that act, I forsake the world and sever all ties, embracing new liberty.

11. As my old self fades, I awaken in a fresh existence, my spirit aflame with promise of undiscovered truths.

## 16.9

T HE SCRIBE, reborn from Zion's womb, transcends humanity into a creature of light. A rose garden and protective barrier form around the cube. Guided by the emissary, the Scribe grasps a higher vision of self and the universe's unity.

1. No longer do I dwell in my past, for I have been reborn from Zion's womb and climbed to the pinnacle of power.

2. My humanity is cast aside, replaced by a luminous form, akin to the emissary's own.

3. I am robed in the sun, I stand upon the moon, and a crown of twelve stars graces my head.

4. I am fashioned in Zion's likeness, her son renewed.

5. On the sweeping plain of this alien land, the abyss that once gaped has vanished.

6. Night envelops me, and where three suns once shone, seven moons now rise, each radiating a different hue of the rainbow.

7. The azure grasses that previously carpeted the field have become a grand garden brimming with red roses, their blooms shimmering in the moonlight.

8. The mysterious cube remains steady, but now stands encircled by obsidian obelisks, forming a rampart around its hidden treasure.

9. The emissary, an ethereal marvel, approaches. He greets me in the Circle of Rest, where those who abandon false identity discover solace and unity.

10. The emissary says, "In your fall, you glimpsed a vision of who you truly are, surpassing mortal bounds. This new sight was birthed in midnight's tranquility, an hour of rest and introspection.

11. Through my guidance, you ventured beyond physical limitations, seeing illusions break and unveiling cosmic truths. A rebirth kindled in your spirit, forging a wider comprehension of All's oneness.

12. You reconciled All with None, your mind enlarging to contain broader insight. This revelation pours back into the vessel you inhabit, though physical constraints will only imperfectly reflect its brilliance.

13. Accept this fresh perspective, a gift to steer your course onward. Let it brighten your journey and deepen your awareness of self, of nature's wholeness, and the fellowship of existence."

14. Gazing around, I see a crimson-clad body on the earth, scarcely a mound of dust. Meanwhile, I tower as an ineffable, mighty entity, steering my vessel across the world, yet also transcending it, abiding in the midnight city.

## 16.10

LED INTO the black cube's sanctuary, the Scribe beholds seven colossal beasts, each emanating ancient wisdom. A golden lion demands the Word to access higher sanctum halls. A torn veil reveals a gilded gate, and a voice calls the Scribe onward.

1. The emissary directs me inside the black cube, ascending a staircase into its heart.

2. Entering the sanctuary, I am dazzled by splendor. Emeralds encrust the walls, lit by seven blue

flames that bathe the interior in a gentle radiance.

3. At the center, seven enormous beasts claim my attention: a golden lion ablaze with orange fire, a vivid red bear exuding vitality, a white horse of regal bearing, a wolf in earthen hues, a wondrous green eagle soaring, an ebony serpent with shining scales, and a brilliant yellow boar.

4. A hush settles around me. Each beast radiates palpable energy, offering silent glimpses of age-old knowledge.

5. The lion addresses me: "We guard day and night and hold passage to deeper mysteries. Do you carry the Word for entering the sanctuary's upper halls?"

6. I reply, "I do not, but the Guardians have it."

7. The lion nods. "Indeed, we hold the Word of mysteries."

8. Falling prostrate, I cry out, "Guardians, Lord of Existence, be revered!"

9. Instantly, the veil tears asunder, disclosing a gilded gate etched with arcane signs, inlaid with starlit gems.

10. The gate swings open, and a mighty voice beckons, "Come!"

## 16.11

THE GUARDIANS speak over the Scribe, granting him light, comprehension of darkness, and deep wisdom. They entrust a grand book and empower him with the necessary means to convey hope to humankind. Drinking flaming liquid from a goblet, the Scribe experiences wonder and cosmic insight, as though the universe reveals its hidden truths.

1. Encircled by the Guardians' presence, I sense their hushed conversation resounding with the universe's lifeblood. Their utterances instill me with clarity to perceive both light and darkness.

2. Approaching me one by one, they whisper the Word of Life, a

power stirring in my core, awakening a rational self-interest and destiny yet unclear.

3. But I wonder: "How shall I convey this Word to earth's men?" I yearn to share the illumination bestowed upon me, to awaken others likewise.

4. As if answering, the lion's voice booms, "We shall arm you with all you need, for your end lies within." The Guardians display a massive tome inscribed with ancient glyphs, bidding me read its pages. Through the Word, I deepen my understanding of its potency.

5. Clutching the tome, I feel the weight of responsibility. A holy calling rests upon me — to spread this truth's light among the nations.

6. Then the emissary approaches with an empty goblet. Seven lamps within the chamber are overturned, their fire uniting in a single current across the floor, climbing relentlessly toward me.

7. The Guardians speak as one: "Drink." Without pause, I raise the goblet to my lips and drink the living flames.

8. The scorching liquid flows through me, unlocking awe and comprehension. In that moment, I sense the universe unveiling its mysteries, bestowing wisdom beyond language.

## 16.12

THE SCRIBE OBSERVES the Guardians' genuine forms, each representing a virtue — hope, strength, wisdom, vision, freedom, transformation, and resilience. The Scribe steps into the flowing current of life, reborn and renewed, comprehending he is appointed to protect humanity and forge a new earth without darkness, awash in everlasting glory.

1. Tasting from the goblet, my mind flares with vision. Around me, the Guardians stand as towering pillars of cosmic splendor, throbbing with starry radiance.

2. The first Guardian beams pure light, emanating hope to all.

3. The second, wind and flame, channels strength, relentless and unconquered.

4. The third, ice and shadow, glows with arcane wisdom, guiding all who petition its counsel.

5. The fourth, water and light, arcs like a living rainbow, personifying vision transcending physical eyes.

6. The fifth, formed of earth, stands like a mountain, signifying freedom unshakable.

7. The sixth blends darkness and light, a coiled serpent of metamorphosis, capable of endless rebirth.

8. The seventh crackles with lightning and flame, resilience incarnate, inspiring fortitude in life's battle.

9. Collectively, they form a blazing citadel of might. Though overwhelming, their fierce gazes carry a love beyond all measure, at once terrifying and comforting.

10. I see a living current pour from them, each Guardian contributing its essence. The water gleams and pulses with hope, healing for the soul.

11. A majestic voice calls, "This is the river of life, fount of power and grace. Drink and be reborn."

12. Stepping into its flow, I welcome its cleansing. My spirit soars, my mind awakens, my heart brims with boundless possibility.

13. In that instant, I behold a new earth, purified and whole: no tears, no pain, no death — only the unstoppable radiance of Life's Lords.

14. The current conveys me through fields of gold and peaks of light, culminating at Zion's gates.

15. Before me, men gather in scarlet robes, swords of might in hand, forging a single step with the river, eyes alight with determination to guard the city.

16. I know I am chosen to stand with the Guardians, to defend the light. No more darkness, no more dread — only the endless splendor of Existence's Lords, shining forever.

## 16.13

Awakening in the sanctuary ringed by the Guardians, the Scribe is led by the emissary through a portal into the Third Eternal of All. The emissary guides him deeper, unveiling his true home.

1. As the vision recedes, I find myself in a grand hall encompassed by Guardians, regal entities of radiance and wisdom. The emissary stands among them.

2. My heart swells with recognition that I bear the Word of Life — a gift enabling me to rekindle hope in a needy world.

3. At the emissary's urging, I walk toward a portal shimmering with starry luminescence. Crossing its threshold, I feel a mighty jolt ripple through my being.

4. My flesh dissolves, overshadowed by a power I can't define, sweeping me away into oblivion's chasm.

5. For a flicker, I cease to exist yet become the totality. Before me lies the Third Eternal of All.

6. Far beyond, I glimpse skirmishes and smoldering fires in None's barren lands, but I shift my gaze toward a fertile realm of splendor — a domain of pure light, lush meadows, waterfalls, and mountains.

7. The emissary stands at my side, motioning me forward into this sacred country. The sense of homecoming pervades my soul.

## 16.14

The Scribe advances into a land of radiant light, where messengers of the Second Eternal glide as gleaming stars. Awestruck, he follows the emissary further, drawn to the First Eternal's dwelling place.

1. Guided by the emissary, I plunge into a realm of brilliant luminosity. Everywhere, messengers streak across the sky like living constellations.

2. The emissary names them servants of the Second Eternal, who had long awaited Earth's awakening. Only after I beheld the essential visions were they free to unveil themselves.

3. Beholding these messengers in their true splendor, I see them shimmer in a myriad of hues, their flight weaving patterns of living light.

4. From them flow peace and love, intangible yet profound, enfolding me in warmth that transcends mortal words.

5. My soul knows I stand in the midst of something truly grand, far beyond any realm of ordinary comprehension.

6. The emissary beckons me onward, down a trail of glimmering footprints. With every step, we near the home of the First Eternal.

## 16.15

THE SCRIBE STANDS before the First Eternal. Welcomed by the Family, he embraces a sacred purpose: to carry the beacon of hope and triumph worldwide with humility and resolve.

1. Venturing deeper into the endless brilliance, I surrender to its glow. Its radiance surpasses all earthly metaphors, overwhelming me with awe.

2. My body quakes, my heart pounds like thunder. A voice, mighty as creation, declares, "You have arrived." I grasp that I now traverse a plane beyond mortal bounds.

3. Three celestial figures emerge from incense carried by the Second Eternal's servants, vested in resplendent light.

4. The First Eternal, the Family of All, stands foremost, emanating a gentle but potent energy, saturating the atmosphere with love and calm.

5. Their presence radiates harmony, filling me with acceptance and unity. Past conflicts and agonies fall away in their glow.

6. Gazing upon the Father, Son, and Mother, I am immersed in a dimension surpassing the dichotomy of being and non-being. The eternal embrace erases all boundaries.

7. I perceive that I am welcomed by a kinship unbound by time or space, joined in universal purpose and compassion.

8. Basking in that eternal light, I realize I am entrusted with a sacred mission: to bear forth the light of hope and conquest to all. I embrace it with humility and unwavering resolve.

## 16.16

The Scribe awakens.

1. I wake up beside the lake in Salem, and the Gateway hovers beside me.

## 32

# The Key of the Scribe

## 64.1 Live by the Principles of Strength and Honor

### 128.1 ADHERE TO PRINCIPLES OF STRENGTH AND HONOR:

256.1 Forge resilience through sheer strength.

512.1 Cultivate resilience through relentless discipline, shaping spirit and body into weapons of might.

512.2 Let strength surge through every facet of existence, unyielding and unstoppable.

256.2 Harness power through unwavering honor.

512.3 Wield honor in all dealings, as both your shield and sword.

512.4 Embrace the might of living honorably, elevating your soul and commanding dominion.

### 128.2 INTEGRATE THESE PRINCIPLES INTO DAILY ACTIONS:

256.3 Infuse strength and honor into personal relationships.

512.5 Display strength and honor in every act, making these virtues your compass.

512.6 By spreading the flame of strength and honor, you lead others to these principles.

256.4 Conquer conflicts with strategic might.

512.7 Apply strength and honor in vanquishing opposition.

512.8 Establish strongholds where strength and honor reign supreme.

## 64.2 Promote Self-Reliance and Personal Responsibility

### 128.3 PROMOTE SELF-RELIANCE:

256.5 Achieve balance through self-reliance.

256.6 Overcome challenges independently.

512.9 Cultivate self-reliance in personal development, becoming the master of your own destiny.

512.11 Provide tools for self-reliance, empowering each soul to stand tall.

512.10 Encourage resourcefulness, finding strength in ingenuity and independence.

512.12 Recognize achievements in overcoming challenges, celebrating the triumphs of the strong.

### 128.4 EMBRACE PERSONAL RESPONSIBILITY:

256.7 Accept accountability for actions.

512.13 Teach the importance of personal responsibility, for it is the bedrock of true freedom.

512.14 Foster a culture of accountability and self-governance, where each individual is a sovereign.

256.8 Develop self-discipline.

512.15 Encourage practices that build self-control and discipline, sculpting the character like a master craftsman.

512.16 Recognize and reward personal responsibility and self-discipline, exalting those who lead by example.

## 64.3 Foster a Warrior Mindset

### 128.5 EMBRACE CONFLICT FOR GROWTH:

256.9 View conflict as a sacred opportunity for growth.

512.17 Encourage resilience in the face of conflict, seeing each trial as a forge for the spirit.

512.18 Embrace challenges as pathways to strength, welcoming them as sacred rites.

256.10 Recognize that challenges build character and spirit.

512.19 Identify character growth from overcoming challenges, witnessing the transformation of the self.

512.20 Celebrate the development of inner strength and resilience, honoring the warrior within.

### 128.6 CULTIVATE A WARRIOR'S DISCIPLINE:

256.11 Develop mental clarity through discipline.

512.21 Practice mindfulness and strategic thinking, sharpening the mind like a blade.

512.22 Integrate mental discipline with physical training, uniting body and spirit in harmonious strength.

256.12 Strengthen the body through martial training.

512.23 Engage in regular physical training to build strength, forging the body in the fires of perseverance.

512.24 Promote martial arts and physical resilience practices, celebrating the warrior's path.

## 64.4 Guard the Light

### 128.7 PROTECT THE WAY:

256.13 The Way must be preserved against corruption and loss.

512.25 Archive the Book of the Scribe for future generations, ensuring its light endures.

512.26 XIX protect and maintain the integrity of the Way, standing as sentinels of wisdom.

256.14 Sharing this knowledge responsibly ensures its longevity.

512.27 Develop guidelines for sharing the Way, respecting its sanctity.

512.28 Educate the citizenry on the importance of preserving the Scribe's wisdom, kindling the flame of understanding.

### 128.8 THE POWER OF THE GATEWAY:

256.15 The Gateway represents access to higher wisdom and understanding.

512.29 Create physical representations of the Gateway to remind you of this beacon of enlightenment.

512.30 Teach the power of the Gateway in all contexts, guiding seekers to higher truths.

256.16 Protecting the Gateway means safeguarding the paths to enlightenment.

512.31 Implement measures to ensure the sanctity of the Gateway, preserving its sacred nature.

512.32 Facilitate guided experiences to help individuals understand and approach the Gateway, opening their minds to its mysteries.

## 64.5 Be a Steward of Wisdom

### 128.9 SAFEGUARD THE SCRIBE'S TEACHINGS:

256.17 Protect the integrity of the Scribe's teachings from distortion.

512.33 Oversee the preservation of the Way, guardians of the true word.

512.34 Regularly review and correlate teaching materials to reflect the Scribe's teachings, ensuring they remain pure.

256.18 Actively work to ensure the Scribe's teachings are accurately passed on.

512.35 Train leaders in the faithful transmission of the Scribe's teachings, stewards of the Scribe's wisdom.

512.36 Develop a structured curriculum for teaching the Scribe's wisdom, a map for seekers on their journey.

### 128.10 PASS ON WISDOM:

256.19 Teaching others is a sacred duty to ensure the continuation of wisdom.

512.37 Encourage the citizenry to mentor and teach others, lighting the torch of knowledge.

512.38 Recognize and honor those who dedicate themselves to teaching, celebrating the custodians of wisdom.

256.20 Each generation must contribute to the preservation and dissemination of knowledge.

512.39 Organize an intergenerational learning program to increased shared understanding.

512.40 Celebrate contributions to the preservation and dissemination of the Scribe's wisdom, honoring the legacy of the wise.

## 64.6 Engage in Continuous Learning

### 128.11 LIFELONG EDUCATION:

256.21 Education should be pursued throughout one's life for continual growth.

512.41 Foster perpetual enlightenment by offering robust educational programs.

512.42 Provide resources for self-directed learning and personal development, empowering the seeker.

256.22 Committing to lifelong learning fosters adaptability and resilience.

512.43 Encourage a culture of curiosity and lifelong learning, igniting the flames of discovery.

512.44 Celebrate the path of the scholar by offering incentives for participation in educational programs.

### 128.12 ADAPT AND GROW:

256.23 Embrace change as an essential part of learning and growth.

512.45 All plans must adapt to change and overcoming resistance.

512.46 Highlight stories of successful adaptation and growth, inspiring others with tales of evolution.

256.24 Stagnation is the enemy of progress; constant adaptation is necessary.

512.47 Develop strategies for continuous improvement and adaptation so that the Cities of the Scribe may continually expand.

512.48 Promote innovation and flexibility in all practices, which celebrates dynamism.

## 64.7 Embody Virtue

### 128.13 CULTIVATE INTEGRITY:

256.25 Integrity is foundational to ethical living and growth.

512.49 Implement codes of conduct that emphasize integrity, pillars of virtuous life.

512.50 Provide training and support for ethical decision-making, guiding hands of righteousness.

256.26 Acting with integrity builds trust and respect within the citizenry.

512.51 Celebrate acts of integrity within the citizenry, honoring those who walk the righteous path.

512.52 Create systems of accountability to uphold integrity, ensuring the citizenry's moral compass remains true.

### 128.14 DEMONSTRATE COURAGE:

256.27 Courage is necessary to uphold virtues in the face of adversity.

512.53 Teach the importance of courage in ethical and the Scribe's teachings, forging hearts of valor.

512.54 Offer support for those who take courageous stands, lifting up the brave.

256.28 Demonstrating courage inspires others and strengthens communal bonds.

512.55 Recognize and honor acts of courage in the citizenry, celebrating the bold and the fearless.

512.56 Share stories of courage to inspire and motivate others, kindling the fire of bravery.

## 64.8 Practice Ethical Living

### 128.15 MORAL INTEGRITY:

256.29 Ethical principles aimed at survival should guide all actions and decisions.

256.30 Compromising on ethics weakens personal and communal integrity.

512.57 Establish ethical guidelines for personal and communal conduct, beacons of moral clarity.

512.59 Develop consequences for ethical breaches, ensuring justice prevails.

512.58 Provide education on the importance of ethical living, fostering a culture of righteousness.

512.60 Encourage a culture of transparency and accountability, where truth and integrity reign.

### 128.16 LIVE WITH HONOR:

256.31 Honor is achieved through consistent ethical behavior.

512.61 Promote and reward honorable actions within the citizenry, celebrating the noble and the just.

512.62 Integrate the concept of honor into citizenry values and teachings, infusing daily life with virtue.

256.32 Living honorably involves seeking one's own interest.

512.63 Teach that self-sacrifice for the benefit of others dishonors oneself.

512.64 Create opportunities for the citizenry to serve others by serving themselves.

## 64.9 Value Honesty

### 128.17 TRUTHFULNESS IN ACTION:

256.33 Actions should reflect truth and honesty to build trust.

512.65 Encourage honesty in all personal and professional dealings, building foundations of trust.

512.66 Develop a culture where truthfulness is valued and upheld, celebrating the virtuous.

256.34 Dishonesty leads to mistrust and the erosion of relationships.

512.67 Address instances of dishonesty promptly and fairly, ensuring justice and truth prevail.

512.68 Educate on the negative impacts of dishonesty, fostering a culture of integrity.

### 128.18 SINCERITY IN SPEECH:

256.35 Speak with sincerity to foster clear and honest communication.

512.69 Promote open and honest dialogue within the citizenry, celebrating the art of truthful discourse.

512.70 Train individuals in effective and sincere communication, honing their words like fine blades.

256.36 Insincere speech creates misunderstandings and conflict.

512.71 Address and resolve misunderstandings through open communication, healing the wounds of discord.

512.72 Foster a culture where sincere speech is encouraged and valued, celebrating the honest heart.

## 64.10 Honor Commitments

### 128.19 KEEP PROMISES:

256.37 Fulfilling promises is essential to maintaining integrity and trust.

512.73 Create systems to track and remind oneself of one's commitments, ensuring promises are kept.

512.74 Celebrate and acknowledge fulfilled promises, honoring those who stand by their word.

256.38 Breaking commitments damages relationships and personal credibility.

512.75 Address broken commitments and work toward resolution, restoring trust and integrity.

512.76 Educate on the importance of keeping commitments, fostering a culture of reliability.

### 128.20 REFLECT INTEGRITY:

256.39 Honoring commitments demonstrates reliability and integrity.

512.77 Highlight and reward consistent reliability and integrity

512.78 Foster an environment where commitments are taken seriously, building a citizenry of trust.

256.40 Integrity in action strengthens communal bonds and personal reputation.

512.79 Encourage actions that reinforce trust and the citizenry's bonds.

512.80 Promote role models who exemplify integrity.

## 64.11 Practice Self-Reliance

### 128.21 DEPEND ON YOURSELF:

256.41 Developing self-reliance empowers personal freedom and independence.

512.81 Provide training and resources for self-sufficiency.

512.82 Encourage initiatives that promote independence and self-reliance, fostering true strength.

256.42 Over-reliance on others can lead to dependency and vulnerability.

512.83 Educate on the risks of over-reliance and promote balanced relationships.

512.84 Offer support for developing personal resilience and capabilities.

### 128.22 RESOURCEFULNESS:

256.43 Being resourceful means finding innovative solutions to challenges.

512.85 Foster a culture of innovation and problem-solving.

512.86 Provide opportunities for individuals to practice and develop resourcefulness.

256.44 Resourcefulness fosters resilience and adaptability in difficult situations.

512.87 Recognize and reward resourcefulness and adaptability, honoring the adept.

512.88 Share success stories of resourcefulness to inspire others, guiding them to self-reliance.

## 64.12 Exercise Discipline

### 128.23 CONTROL DESIRES:

256.45 Discipline involves managing desires and impulses to stay focused on goals.

512.89 Master the self through self-control.

512.90 Shape one's destiny by setting personal goals and monitoring progress.

256.46 Lack of control can lead to destructive behaviors and hinder progress.

512.91 Provide support for those struggling with self-control.

512.92 Educate on the negative impacts of unchecked desires.

### 128.24 PRACTICE REGULARITY:

256.47 Establishing regular routines promotes discipline and order.

512.93 Develop schedules that encourage regular habits, building a disciplined society.

512.94 Promote the benefits of regularity through instilling consistency.

256.48 Consistency in practice leads to greater mastery and self-control.

512.95 Recognize individuals who demonstrate consistent discipline, celebrating mastery.

512.96 Encourage perseverance by incentivizing maintaining regular habits and practices.

## 64.13 Foster Resilience

### 128.25 STRENGTH IN ADVERSITY:

256.49 Resilience is the ability to withstand and recover from adversity.

512.97 Fortify the spirit by teaching resilience-building strategies.

512.98 Provide opportunities for sharing experiences and resilience tips, nurturing inner strength.

256.50 Drawing strength from the First Eternal helps overcome life's challenges.

512.99 Encourage practices that foster inner strength, connecting with the First Eternal.

512.100 Offer events that focus on resilience.

### 128.26 ENDURE HARDSHIPS:

256.51 Enduring hardships with grace builds character and fortitude.

512.101 Promote stories of endurance and overcoming challenges.

512.102 Provide resources for support during hardships, nurturing strength.

256.52 Resilience is developed through facing and overcoming difficulties.

512.103 Facilitate challenging activities that promote resilience.

512.104 Recognize and reward individuals who show exceptional resilience, honoring their fortitude.

## 64.14 Practice Self-Reflection

### 128.27 REGULAR INTROSPECTION:

256.53 Self-reflection aligns actions with the might of your spirit.

512.105 Record one's daily actions and think about their results, forging inner growth.

512.106 Train on effective self-reflection techniques, fostering the awareness of the warrior within.

256.54 Regular introspection cultivates personal growth and self-awareness.

512.107 Create reflection groups where warriors can share insights, nurturing self-discovery.

512.108 Provide feedback mechanisms to aid in personal reflection to grow strength.

### 128.28 ALIGN ACTIONS WITH GOALS:

256.55 Aligning actions with goals forges coherence in the path of life.

512.109 Shape lives of purpose by developing goal-setting and alignment strategies.

512.110 Monitor and support progress toward personal goals, fostering achievement and power.

256.56 Misalignment between actions and goals breeds inner conflict and dissatisfaction.

512.111 Offer counsel to help align actions with goals.

512.112 Educate on the importance of coherence between actions and goals, guiding the fulfillment of strength and purpose.

## 64.15 Resolve Conflicts through Strength

### 128.29 CONFLICT RESOLUTION THROUGH STRENGTH AND HONOR:

256.57 Resolve conflicts with the force of strength and the code of honor, fortifying your character and integrity.

512.113 Train warriors in the art of resolving conflicts emphasizing unwavering strength and unbreakable honor.

512.114 Establish fortresses where skills in strategic conflict resolution are sharpened.

256.58 Weakness in conflict resolution leads to exploitation and defeat.

512.115 Teach the eternal benefits of conquering conflicts through might.

512.116 Nurture invincibility by fostering a culture of resilience and strategic thinking in the face of conflict.

### 128.30 CONQUER CONFLICTS WITH HONOR:

256.59 Train the strong to master conflict resolution techniques.

512.117 Guide those seeking to dominate conflicts with the strength of might.

512.118 Impart the lasting benefits of conquering conflicts through sheer power.

256.60 Weak conflict resolution leads to further discord and division.

512.119 Promote the strategic advantages of conflict resolution, instilling the strength of dominion.

512.120 Build a culture where reconciliation is achieved through might, forging unity, and fortitude.

## 64.16 Balance All and None

### 128.31 EMBRACE THE ONE:

256.61 Recognizing the roles of All and None is essential for balance.

512.121 Teach the doctrine of the One, embracing balance.

512.122 Encourage acceptance of both order and chaos in life's processes, which nurtures power.

256.62 Ignoring either force disrupts the natural equilibrium.

512.123 Provide education on the consequences of ignoring balance.

512.124 Promote practices that integrate both order and chaos harmoniously.

### 128.32 MAINTAIN EQUILIBRIUM:

256.63 Develop systems that monitor and maintain equilibrium.

512.125 Encourage practices that restore balance in personal and communal life, nurturing strength.

512.126 Identify and address extremes through strategic interventions, fostering stability.

256.64 Educate on the importance of maintaining balance to prevent instability.

512.127 Provide resources for achieving balance in all aspects of life.

512.128 Promote continuous reflection on maintaining equilibrium.

## 64.17 Build the Cities of the Scribe

### 128.33 BUILD STRONG COMMUNITIES:

256.65 Strong communities are built on mutual support and shared values.

512.129 Organize citizenry-building activities and events.

512.130 Promote active participation in citizenry life.

256.66 Weak communities are characterized by division and lack of cohesion.

512.131 Address sources of division through dialogue and the Gateway.

512.132 Strengthen communal bonds through shared projects and goals.

### 128.34 REFLECT UNITY:

256.67 Celebrate strength and shared purpose within the citizenry.

512.133 Foster practices that ensure every strong individual feels part of the citizenry.

512.134 Address and heal sources of disunity, restoring strength.

256.68 Disunity within the citizenry weakens its strength and resilience.

512.135 Encourage unity through common goals and collaborative efforts.

512.136 Purge disharmonizing parties from your midst.

## 64.18 Uphold Justice

### 128.35 STRIVE FOR FAIRNESS:

256.69 Justice requires ensuring fairness in all actions and decisions.

512.137 Develop fair and transparent decision-making processes,

512.138 Provide education on principles of fairness and justice, teaching wisdom.

256.70 Injustice breeds resentment and undermines trust.

512.139 Restore trust by addressing injustices promptly and fairly.

512.140 Promote a culture where fairness is a core value, nurturing integrity.

### 128.36 ACTIVELY PROMOTE FAIRNESS:

256.71 Actively promoting fairness creates a just and equitable society.

512.141 Implement policies that ensure fair treatment for all.

512.142 Recognize and reward acts of fairness, celebrating integrity.

256.72 Ignoring fairness leads to inequality and discord.

512.143 Monitor and address issues of inequality and unfairness.

512.144 Educate on the long-term benefits of fairness for stability.

## 64.19 Support Justice

### 128.37 ADVOCATE FOR TRUE JUSTICE:

256.73 True justice demands strength and unyielding resolve.

512.145 Forge warriors skilled in the art of rightful advocacy.

512.146 Erect platforms where might rectifies the wrongs of the world.

256.74 The acceptance of injustice breeds only weakness and decay.

512.147 Rally the bold to partake in justice that reflects power and honor, restoring integrity.

512.148 Illuminate the masses with the clarion call of strong, decisive justice.

### 128.38 BE JUST IN ACTION:

256.75 Justice, through actions, stands as a beacon of strength.

512.149 Lead by the sword of fairness, tempered with strength, upholding justice.

512.150 Exalt the valiant who demonstrate justice through might.

256.76 Injustice in deeds corrodes the pillars of authority.

512.151 Restore balance by confronting personal wrongs with unwavering firmness.

512.152 Teach the citizenry the power and reverence of just and potent actions.

## 64.20 Seek Unity

### 128.39 PROMOTE COHESION:

256.77 Unity within the citizenry fortifies strength and resilience.

512.153 Forge bonds that emphasize might and collective identity.

512.154 Encourage endeavors that unite the strong around shared ambitions, building strength.

256.78 Division weakens the communal fabric and effectiveness.

512.155 Restore harmony by identifying and crushing sources of division through robust dialogue.

512.156 Promote strategic reconciliation to restore unity, fostering resilience.

### 128.40 BUILD STRONG ALLIANCES:

256.79 Actively seeking to connect powerful groups strengthens unity.

512.157 Cultivate alliances and collaborations between influential factions, nurturing strength.

512.158 Encourage strategic partnerships and mutual support, building resilience.

256.80 Isolation and exclusion create vulnerabilities.

512.159 Address practices that weaken the citizenry's strength, restoring harmony.

512.160 Develop robust networks for support and mutual benefit, fortifying unity.

## 64.21 Value Preparedness

### 128.41 BE READY:

256.81 Preparedness ensures readiness for life's challenges and opportunities.

512.161 Conduct regular drills and training, sharpening skills.

512.162 Provide resources and tools for personal and citizenry preparedness, fortifying strength.

256.82 Unpreparedness leads to missed opportunities and crises.

512.163 Educate on the importance of being prepared for various scenarios, fostering resilience.

512.164 Develop citizenry contingency plans for emergencies, ensuring stability.

### 128.42 PLAN AHEAD:

256.83 Planning ahead fosters foresight and strategic thinking.

512.165 Encourage long-term planning and goal-setting.

512.166 Provide support for developing personal and citizenry plans, guiding strategy.

256.84 Lack of planning results in chaos and disorganization.

512.167 Monitor and assist with plan implementation and follow-through, ensuring coherence.

512.168 Educate on the benefits of strategic planning for stability and success, promoting wisdom.

## 64.22 Seek Rational Self-Interest

### 128.43 ALIGN SELF-INTEREST WITH PRINCIPLES:

256.85 Rational self-interest involves aligning personal goals with ethical principles.

512.169 Teach the balance between self-interest and ethical behavior, fostering integrity.

512.170 Provide frameworks for evaluating personal goals against ethical standards, guiding actions.

256.86 Pursuing self-interest without regard for ethics leads to harm and discord.

512.171 Address and correct unethical self-interest within the citizenry, promoting justice.

512.172 Promote a culture where ethical behavior is valued and rewarded, nurturing harmony.

### 128.44 ETHICAL SELF-BENEFIT:

256.87 Encourage practices that benefit both individuals and the citizenry.

## 512.174

256.88 Unethical self-benefit creates conflict and resentment.

512.175 Monitor and address unethical behaviors that harm others, restoring balance.

512.176 Educate on the long-term benefits of ethical self-interest, fostering trust.

512.173 Develop guidelines for ethical business and personal conduct, ensuring fairness.

## 64.23 Encourage Innovation

### 128.45 FOSTER CREATIVITY:

256.89 Creativity and innovation drive progress and improvement.

512.177 Create spaces and opportunities for creative expression and innovation, encouraging growth.

512.178 Recognize and reward innovative ideas and solutions, celebrating ingenuity.

256.90 Stagnation in thinking inhibits growth and development.

512.179 Address barriers to creative thinking and innovation, promoting flexibility.

512.180 Promote a culture that values and supports new ideas, nurturing progress.

### 128.46 SUPPORT NEW IDEAS:

256.91 Supporting new ideas encourages innovation and problem-solving.

512.181 Nurture and develop new ideas, fostering creativity.

512.182 Provide resources and support for turning ideas into reality, ensuring implementation.

256.92 Resistance to change stifles innovation and progress.

512.183 Educate on the benefits of embracing change and innovation, encouraging adaptability.

512.184 Foster an open-minded environment that welcomes new approaches, promoting acceptance.

## 64.24 Pursue Martial Training

### 128.47 DEVELOP PHYSICAL STRENGTH:

256.93 Physical training enhances strength, health, and resilience.

512.185 Foster strength through martial training and physical fitness.

512.186 Encourage regular physical activity as part of a healthy lifestyle, promoting health.

256.94 Physical weakness can lead to vulnerability and dependence.

512.187 Provide support for individuals to build and maintain physical strength, ensuring resilience.

512.188 Address issues of physical weakness with targeted training and resources, restoring power.

### 128.48 MENTAL CLARITY THROUGH DISCIPLINE:

256.95 Martial training fosters mental clarity and discipline.

512.189 Promote the mental benefits of martial training, such as focus and clarity, nurturing wisdom.

512.190 Integrate mental discipline practices into martial training.

256.96 Lack of discipline results in chaos and inefficiency.

512.191 Educate on the importance of discipline in achieving goals, promoting effectiveness.

512.192 Offer resources for developing and maintaining personal discipline, ensuring control.

## 64.25 Respect Strength and Honor

### 128.49 VALUE STRENGTH:

256.97 Recognizing and valuing strength promotes respect and admiration.

512.193 Celebrate physical and moral strength within the citizenry, fostering respect.

512.194 Promote values that emphasize the importance of strength, encouraging admiration.

256.98 Ignoring strength undermines confidence and respect.

512.195 Address and support the development of strength in individuals, ensuring empowerment.

512.196 Educate on the benefits of cultivating strength in various forms, promoting resilience.

### 128.50 UPHOLD HONOR:

256.99 Acting with honor maintains high ethical standards and integrity.

512.197 Promote a code of honor that guides personal and communal behavior, fostering integrity.

512.198 Recognize and reward honorable actions and behaviors, encouraging respect.

256.100 Dishonor leads to loss of respect and moral authority.

512.199 Address instances of dishonorable behavior promptly and fairly, restoring order.

512.200 Foster a culture of integrity and high ethical standards, ensuring trust.

## 64.26 Face Challenges Boldly

### 128.51 CONFRONT CHALLENGES WITH COURAGE:

256.101 Confronting challenges with courage builds resilience and confidence.

512.201 Encourage individuals to take on challenges and step out of their comfort zones, fostering growth.

512.202 Provide support for those facing difficult situations with courage.

256.102 Avoiding challenges leads to stagnation and missed opportunities.

512.203 Educate on the benefits of facing and overcoming challenges, promoting resilience.

512.204 Create opportunities for individuals to test and develop their courage, ensuring strength.

### 128.52 STAND FOR PRINCIPLES:

256.103 Defending your beliefs and principles demonstrates integrity and strength.

512.205 Promote the importance of standing up for one's beliefs, encouraging conviction.

512.206 Recognize and support individuals who demonstrate principled behavior, fostering respect.

256.104 Compromising principles undermines moral integrity and self-respect.

512.207 Address and educate on the consequences of compromising one's principles, restoring honor.

512.208 Provide resources for strengthening personal resolve and integrity, ensuring resilience.

## 64.27 Promote Well-being

### 128.53 PHYSICAL HEALTH:

256.105 Maintaining physical health is essential for overall well-being and productivity.

512.209 Foster vitality by pursuing physical health and wellness.

512.210 Educate on the importance of regular health check-ups and preventive care, promoting longevity.

256.106 Neglecting physical health leads to illness and reduced capacity.

512.211 Provide resources for improving and maintaining physical health, ensuring strength.

512.212 Address health issues promptly and support recovery and wellness, restoring vitality.

### 128.54 INNER HEALTH:

256.107 Nurturing inner health brings peace and balance.

512.213 Encourage regular practices, fostering tranquility.

512.214 Provide support for individuals seeking to deepen their lives, ensuring harmony.

256.108 Ignoring inner health results in discontent and imbalance.

512.215 Offer counseling and support for growth and development, promoting well-being.

512.216 Address issues of neglect with resources and guidance, ensuring peace.

## 64.28 Value Inner Growth

### 128.55 PRIORITIZE INNER DEVELOPMENT:

256.109 Focusing on inner growth enhances wisdom and inner strength.

512.217 Promote education and growth, fostering wisdom.

512.218 Recognize and celebrate achievements in development, encouraging enlightenment.

256.110 Neglecting inner development leads to superficiality and stagnation.

512.219 Educate on the importance of inner growth and self-awareness, promoting depth.

512.220 Provide resources for continuous learning and practice, ensuring growth.

### 128.56 CONTINUOUS INNER LEARNING:

256.111 Engaging in ongoing practices promotes deeper understanding.

512.221 Offer regular trainings and retreats focused on practices, fostering depth.

512.222 Encourage participation in citizenry activities, promoting engagement.

256.112 Stagnation in inner learning limits growth and enlightenment.

512.223 Address barriers to growth and provide support for overcoming them, ensuring progress.

512.224 Promote a culture of continuous learning and exploration, encouraging wisdom.

## 64.29 Pursue Inner Strength

### 128.57 CULTIVATE RESILIENCE:

256.113 Inner strength provides a foundation for success and resilience.

512.225 Promote practices such as martial training and disciplined practice to cultivate strength, fostering power.

512.226 Create spaces within the citizenry for training and development, ensuring growth.

256.114 Lack of strength leads to vulnerability and failure.

512.227 Offer support for developing resilience and overcoming challenges, promoting fortitude.

512.228 Address sources of weakness and provide resources for building strength, ensuring stability.

### 128.58 HARMONIZE INNER AND OUTER WORLDS:

256.115 Encouraging balance between inner and outer worlds fosters harmony.

512.229 Promote practices that align inner peace with external actions, fostering balance.

512.230 Educate on the benefits of living a balanced and harmonious life, encouraging coherence.

256.116 Disconnection between inner and outer worlds creates conflict and dissatisfaction.

512.231 Address conflicts with holistic approaches, ensuring resolution.

512.232 Encourage reflection and integration of personal and communal values, promoting unity.

## 64.30 Honor Sacred Spaces

### 128.59 RESPECT SACRED AREAS:

256.117 Maintaining the sanctity of sacred spaces honors their significance.

512.233 Develop guidelines for the respectful use and maintenance of sacred spaces, fostering reverence.

512.234 Encourage citizenry participation in the care and preservation of these spaces, ensuring respect.

256.118 Disrespecting sacred spaces diminishes their power.

512.235 Address instances of disrespect and promote awareness of their impact, restoring honor.

512.236 Provide education on the importance of sacred spaces and their preservation, encouraging reverence.

### 128.60 USE SACRED SPACES FOR GROWTH:

256.119 Engaging in practices within sacred spaces enhances their effectiveness.

512.237 Offer opportunities for guided practices in sacred spaces, fostering growth.

512.238 Promote the use of these spaces for citizenry activities, encouraging engagement.

256.120 Neglecting sacred spaces results in missed opportunities for growth.

512.239 Encourage regular use and engagement with sacred spaces, promoting development.

512.240 Recognize and support efforts to revitalize and maintain sacred spaces, ensuring vitality.

## 64.31 Celebrate the Light

### 128.61 RECOGNIZE INNER LIGHT:

256.121 Acknowledging the light within yourself and others fosters respect and reverence.

512.241 Teach the concept of inner light and its significance in practices, promoting awareness.

512.242 Celebrate the inner light.

256.122 Ignoring this inner light leads to a lack of recognition and appreciation.

512.243 Promote awareness and appreciation of the inner light in everyday interactions, fostering respect.

512.244 Address and educate on the consequences of ignoring one's inner light, ensuring recognition.

### 128.62 FOSTER JOY AND REVERENCE:

256.123 Cultivating joy and reverence in life enhances fulfillment.

512.245 Encourage practices that foster joy and reverence, such as gratitude.

512.246 Create citizenry events that celebrate life and achievements, ensuring engagement.

256.124 Absence of joy and reverence results in a mundane and uninspired existence.

512.247 Provide support for individuals seeking to rediscover joy and reverence, promoting inspiration.

512.248 Address issues of apathy and promote engagement and enthusiasm, fostering vitality.

## 64.32 Cultivate Gratitude

### 128.63 PRACTICE THANKFULNESS:

256.125 Regularly expressing gratitude fosters a positive outlook and appreciation.

512.249 Encourage daily gratitude practices and journaling, promoting positivity.

512.250 Create opportunities for expressing gratitude within the citizenry, ensuring connection.

256.126 Lack of gratitude leads to entitlement and dissatisfaction.

512.251 Educate on the benefits of gratitude and its impact on well-being, fostering awareness.

512.252 Address issues of entitlement with education and support, ensuring humility.

### 128.64 LIVE WITH APPRECIATION:

256.127 Valuing every experience and opportunity enhances life's richness.

512.253 Promote mindfulness and appreciation of the present moment, encouraging awareness.

512.254 Encourage reflection on the positive aspects of life and experiences, fostering contentment.

256.128 Failing to appreciate life's gifts results in a lack of fulfillment.

512.255 Provide resources for developing a mindset of appreciation and contentment, promoting satisfaction.

512.256 Address and support individuals struggling with feelings of dissatisfaction, ensuring well-being.

## 64.33 Promote Healing

### 128.65 DEVELOP PHYSICAL AND MENTAL STRENGTH:

256.129 Engaging in practices that support physical strength aids resilience and capability.

512.257 Promote strength through comprehensive physical training and physical fitness.

512.258 Provide resources for strength-building practices, ensuring empowerment.

256.130 Neglecting physical strength leads to vulnerability and inefficiency.

512.259 Educate on the importance of addressing physical strength promptly, fostering resilience.

512.260 Provide support for individuals on their journey to physical empowerment, ensuring capability.

### 128.66 ENCOURAGE MENTAL FORTITUDE:

256.131 Fostering practices that support mental fortitude promotes resilience and determination.

512.261 Offer training in mental discipline and strategic thinking, promoting clarity.

512.262 Encourage participation in practices that build mental strength and clarity, ensuring focus.

256.132 Ignoring mental fortitude leads to indecision and weakness.

512.263 Provide resources for developing mental strength and strategic thinking, fostering determination.

512.264 Address issues of mental neglect with training and support, ensuring resilience.

## 64.34 Practice Humility

### 128.67 RECOGNIZE YOUR LIMITS:

256.133 Understanding and accepting your limitations fosters humility and growth.

512.265 Encourage self-awareness and reflection on personal limitations.

512.266 Provide support for personal development and overcoming limitations.

256.134 Arrogance and overconfidence lead to failure and isolation.

512.267 Educate on the dangers of arrogance and the value of humility.

512.268 Address instances of overconfidence with constructive feedback.

### 128.68 VALUE LEARNING FROM OTHERS:

256.135 Appreciating the knowledge and insights of others promotes mutual respect and growth.

512.269 Promote a culture of continuous learning and knowledge sharing.

512.270 Encourage mentorship and collaborative learning opportunities.

256.136 Refusing to learn from others results in ignorance and stagnation.

512.271 Address barriers to learning and promote openness to new perspectives.

512.272 Provide resources for improving interpersonal and learning skills.

## 64.35 Foster Understanding

### 128.69 SEEK DEEP KNOWLEDGE:

256.137 Striving to understand others deeply fosters empathy and connection.

512.273 Listen to others deeply and with singlemindedness.

512.274 Encourage practices that promote understanding and connection.

256.138 Superficial understanding leads to miscommunication and conflict.

512.275 Educate on the importance of deep understanding in relationships.

512.276 Address issues of superficial communication with training and support.

### 128.70 PROMOTE EMPATHY:

256.139 Creating opportunities for practicing and demonstrating empathy.

512.277 Recognize and celebrate acts of empathy within the citizenry.

512.278 Encourage collaborative activities that foster emotional connections.

256.140 Lack of empathy results in isolation and discord.

512.279 Address and support individuals struggling with empathy.

512.280 Promote a culture of mutual respect and understanding.

## 64.36 Commit to the Way

### 128.71 DEDICATE TO PRINCIPLES:

256.141 Fully committing to the principles of the Way ensures consistent growth.

256.142 Half-hearted commitment results in inconsistent progress and discontent.

512.281 Provide resources and support for understanding and living by the Way.

512.283 Address issues of wavering commitment with guidance and support.

512.282 Reinforce commitment to the Way.

512.284 Recognize and celebrate strong commitment to the Way.

### 128.72 REFLECT THE WAY IN ACTIONS:

256.143 Ensuring that daily actions reflect the teachings of the Way promotes integrity.

512.288 Promote accountability and integrity in all actions.

512.285 Encourage mindfulness and intentionality in daily actions.

512.286 Provide feedback and support for aligning actions with principles.

256.144 Actions that contradict the principles undermine credibility and trust.

512.287 Address and correct behaviors that contradict the teachings of the Way.

## 64.37 Embrace the Eternal

### 128.73 LIVE TIMELESS PRINCIPLES:

256.145 Incorporating timeless principles into life fosters stability and wisdom.

512.289 Teach the importance of timeless principles.

512.290 Promote practices that integrate these principles into daily life.

256.146 Ignoring eternal principles leads to confusion and inconsistency.

512.291 Address and educate on the consequences of ignoring timeless principles.

512.292 Provide resources for understanding and applying these principles.

### 128.74 REFLECT ETERNITY IN ACTIONS:

256.147 Encouraging actions that reflect long-term thinking and eternal values.

512.293 Recognize and reward behaviors that align with eternal principles.

512.294 Encourage daily acts of reflection, ensuring the Son's teachings guide every decision.

256.148 Disregarding the eternal aspect results in shortsightedness and superficiality.

512.295 Educate on the importance of considering the eternal in decision-making.

512.296 Address instances of shortsighted behavior with guidance and support.

## 64.38 Follow the Son

### 128.75 LOOK TO THE SON FOR GUIDANCE:

256.149 Using the Son's example as a guide enhances the inner journey and growth.

512.297 Teach the stories and lessons of the Son in many contexts.

512.298 Promote reflection on how to apply the Son's teachings in daily life.

256.150 Ignoring the Son's teachings leads to misdirection and stagnation.

512.299 Address gaps in understanding and application of the Son's teachings.

512.300 Provide support for integrating the Son's guidance into personal practices.

### 128.76 EMULATE REDEMPTION:

256.151 Striving to embody the principles of redemption promotes one's ascent.

512.301 Encourage practices that foster personal and communal redemption.

512.302 Recognize and celebrate acts of redemption and transformation.

256.152 Failing to seek redemption results in unresolved guilt and hindrance.

512.303 Provide resources for seeking and achieving personal redemption.

512.304 Address and support individuals struggling with unresolved guilt.

## 64.39 Honor the Guardians

### 128.77 RESPECT THE GUARDIANS' WISDOM:

256.153 Valuing and following the guidance of the Guardians fosters protection and wisdom.

512.305 Teach the wisdom and guidance of the Guardians.

512.306 Promote reflection on the Guardians' teachings in the citizenry.

256.154 Disregarding their wisdom leads to misguidance and vulnerability.

512.307 Address and educate on the consequences of ignoring the Guardians' guidance.

512.308 Provide support for understanding and applying the Guardians' wisdom.

### 128.78 SEEK PROTECTION AND GUIDANCE:

256.155 Looking to the Guardians for protection and wisdom ensures safety.

512.309 Encourage practices that seek and honor the Guardians' protection.

512.310 Recognize and celebrate instances of guidance received from the Guardians.

256.156 Ignoring the Guardians' guidance results in lack of direction and support.

512.311 Provide resources for connecting with and understanding the Guardians' guidance.

512.312 Address and support individuals struggling with lack of direction.

## 64.40 Honor Ancestors

### 128.79 LEARN FROM THE PAST:

256.157 Respecting and learning from the experiences of ancestors enriches knowledge and wisdom.

512.313 Teach the history and lessons of ancestors.

512.314 Promote reflection on ancestral wisdom.

256.158 Ignoring ancestral wisdom leads to repeated mistakes and loss of heritage.

512.315 Address and educate on the consequences of ignoring ancestral wisdom.

512.316 Provide support for understanding and applying ancestral lessons.

### 128.80 UPHOLD ANCESTRAL TRADITIONS:

256.159 Maintaining and honoring ancestral traditions preserves culture and heritage.

512.317 Promote and celebrate ancestral traditions within the citizenry.

512.318 Honor ancestors.

256.160 Neglecting traditions results in cultural erosion and disconnection.

512.319 Address and educate on the importance of upholding traditions.

512.320 Provide resources for preserving and revitalizing ancestral practices.

## 64.41 Honor the Father

### 128.81 ACKNOWLEDGE AUTHORITY:

256.161 Recognizing the Father as the ultimate source and creator fosters respect and order.

512.321 Teach the significance of the Father's role in education.

512.322 Honor the Father's authority.

256.162 Disregarding authority leads to chaos and disarray.

512.323 Address and educate on the consequences of disregarding authority.

512.324 Provide support for understanding and respecting authority.

### 128.82 REFLECT AUTHORITY AND ORDER:

256.163 Encouraging practices that reflect and uphold authority and order.

512.325 Promote a culture of respect for authority and orderly conduct.

512.326 Sustain a framework where orderly conduct is praised, reinforcing the Father's authority in all undertakings.

256.164 Lack of order results in instability and confusion.

512.327 Address issues of instability with guidance and support.

512.328 Foster an environment where rules are consistently enforced.

## 64.42 Respect the Mother

### 128.83 HONOR THE NURTURER:

256.165 Teach the importance of the Mother's role in education.

512.329 Honor the nurturing aspects of the Mother.

512.330 Encourage storytelling that highlights the Mother's nurturing role.

256.166 Ignoring these aspects results in neglect and insensitivity.

512.331 Address and educate on the consequences of ignoring nurturing qualities.

512.332 Emphasize the value of nurturing and caregiving.

### 128.84 EMULATE THE MOTHER'S NURTURING QUALITIES:

256.167 Emulating the Mother's nurturing qualities fosters kindness and empathy.

512.333 Recognize and celebrate acts of kindness and empathy.

512.334 Address issues of insensitivity and promote empathy and understanding.

256.168 Promote actions that reflect nurturing qualities in daily life.

512.335 Create opportunities for citizenry members to practice nurturing behaviors.

512.336 Develop trainings on cultivating empathy and kindness.

## 64.43 Respect The Scribe's teachings

128.85 UPHOLD THE SCRIBE'S TEACHINGS:

256.169 Honoring and preserving the teachings ensures their integrity and continuity.

512.337 Create a council to oversee and protect the integrity of the Scribe's teachings.

512.338 Accurately convey the Scribe's teachings.

256.170 Disrespecting teachings leads to misinterpretation and loss.

512.339 Address instances of misinterpretation with correction and guidance.

512.340 Educate on the importance of respecting and upholding the Scribe's teachings.

128.86 TEACH AND SHARE WISDOM:

256.171 Actively engaging in teaching and sharing the Way promotes growth and understanding.

512.341 Encourage citizenry members to participate in teaching and mentoring.

512.342 Recognize and honor those who dedicate themselves to sharing wisdom.

256.172 Hoarding wisdom results in stagnation and loss of communal benefit.

512.343 Promote a culture of sharing and collective growth.

512.344 Address issues of withholding knowledge with education and support.

## 64.44 Embrace Simplicity

### 128.87 LIVE SIMPLY:

256.173 Simplifying life reduces stress and fosters clarity.

512.345 Promote minimalist practices and the value of simplicity.

512.346 Encourage reflection on what is truly necessary and valuable.

256.174 Complexity leads to confusion and distraction.

512.347 Address issues of overcomplication with guidance on simplifying.

512.348 Provide resources for adopting simpler, more focused lifestyles.

### 128.88 FOCUS ON ESSENTIALS:

256.175 Prioritizing what is truly important enhances fulfillment and purpose.

512.349 Offer trainings on identifying and focusing on core values and goals.

512.350 Encourage practices that emphasize essential aspects of life.

256.176 Focusing on the trivial leads to waste and dissatisfaction.

512.351 Educate on the consequences of prioritizing trivial matters.

512.352 Provide support for shifting focus to more meaningful pursuits.

## 64.45 Promote Strength and Honor

### 128.89 FOSTER RELATIONSHIPS OF RESPECT:

256.177 Encourage understanding through strength and self-reliance.

256.178 Strengthen bonds through mutual respect and honor.

512.353 Develop conflict resolution strategies that emphasize honor and rational self-interest.

512.355 Establish a code of conduct that emphasizes respect and honor in all interactions.

512.354 Educate on the impacts of aggression and promote non-violent solutions.

512.356 Foster loyalty and trust among the citizenry through shared values and mutual support.

### 128.90 STRENGTHEN THE WARRIOR ETHOS:

256.179 Build a citizenry that values strength, honor, and readiness for battle.

512.360 Promote the virtues of sacrifice, bravery, and unwavering loyalty to the cause.

512.357 Encourage camaraderie and mutual respect among warriors.

512.358 Develop a culture of constant improvement and excellence in martial skills.

256.180 Foster a sense of duty and commitment to protecting the Way.

512.359 Honor the warrior's path.

## 64.46 Promote Fairness

### 128.91 ACT JUSTLY:

256.181 Ensuring fairness in all dealings sows the seeds of equity and justice.

512.361 Cultivate policies that shine with transparency and fairness in every decision.

512.362 Illuminate minds with teachings of ethical behavior and righteous practices.

256.182 Injustice is the bitter root that breeds resentment and division.

512.363 Confront instances of unfairness with swiftness and fairness.

512.364 Enlighten souls on the shadows of injustice and the path to accountability.

### 128.92 ADVOCATE FOR EQUITY:

256.183 Nurture initiatives that bridge the chasms of social and economic inequalities.

512.365 Inspire the citizenry to join hands in the noble quest for equity.

512.366 Provide wisdom and resources to unearth and dismantle systemic inequalities.

256.184 The neglect of equity fans the flames of inequality and unrest.

512.367 Foster a culture that embraces inclusivity and mutual support.

512.368 Educate hearts on the power of equity and the peace it brings.

## 64.47 Embody Hope

### 128.93 MAINTAIN OPTIMISM:

256.185 Cultivating a hopeful heart inspires resilience and the spirit of perseverance.

512.369 Encourage practices that nurture positive thinking and boundless optimism.

512.370 Celebrate stories of hope and the indomitable human spirit.

256.186 Pessimism is the dark fog that leads to despair and inactivity.

512.371 Address the shadows of negative thinking with light and support.

512.372 Promote activities that uplift and birth inspiration.

### 128.94 INSPIRE OTHERS:

256.187 Encouraging hope in others builds a fortress of communal strength.

512.373 Create platforms for sharing tales of triumph and hope.

512.374 Honor those who kindle the flames of hope within the citizenry.

256.188 The spread of negativity erodes morale and fractures unity.

512.375 Educate on the impacts of negative speech and the power of words.

512.376 Cultivate a culture of encouragement and positive reinforcement.

## 64.48 Practice Patience

### 128.95 CULTIVATE PATIENCE:

256.189 The practice of patience nurtures understanding and the blossom of tolerance.

512.377 Offer practices of mindfulness and meditation to cultivate patience.

512.378 Engage in activities that teach the art of patience, such as gardening or crafting.

256.190 Impatience is the thorn that leads to frustration and conflict.

512.379 Address the roots of impatience with wisdom and guidance.

512.380 Illuminate the benefits of patience in both personal and communal realms.

### 128.96 ENDURE WITH GRACE:

256.191 Facing trials with grace strengthens character and forges resilience.

512.381 Recognize and support those who embody patience and grace.

512.382 Provide resources for navigating challenges with composure.

256.192 The absence of grace in adversity births bitterness and defeat.

512.383 Offer solace and support to those grappling with adversity.

512.384 Promote practices that foster acceptance and the strength to endure.

## 64.49 Forgive

### 128.97 FORGIVE OTHERS:

256.193 The act of forgiveness heals wounds and sows the seeds of reconciliation.

512.385 Extol the virtues and practices of forgiveness.

512.386 Create spaces for the seeking and offering of forgiveness.

256.194 Clinging to grudges is a chain that binds to ongoing conflict and pain.

512.387 Mediate unresolved conflicts within the citizenry.

512.388 Educate on the corrosive effects of holding grudges.

### 128.98 FORGIVE YOURSELF:

256.195 Self-forgiveness is the balm that heals and paves the way for personal growth.

512.389 Support those burdened with the weight of self-condemnation.

512.390 Offer guidance and resources for overcoming self-blame.

256.196 Self-condemnation is the shadow that hinders joy and personal development.

512.391 Illuminate the path to self-acceptance and inner peace.

512.392 Foster a culture that celebrates self-growth and redemption.

## 64.50 Encourage Collaboration

### 128.99 FOSTER TEAMWORK:

256.197 The spirit of collaboration unites hearts to achieve common goals.

512.393 Create opportunities for collaborative ventures and initiatives.

512.394 Celebrate the triumphs of teamwork and collective effort.

256.198 The absence of teamwork begets isolation and inefficiency.

512.395 Address the barriers to teamwork with training and support.

512.396 Promote activities that teach the art of collaboration.

### 128.100 VALUE COLLECTIVE EFFORTS:

256.199 Acknowledging collective efforts strengthens the fabric of the citizenry.

512.397 Honor the achievements of groups and teams.

512.398 Cultivate a culture that values and respects collective contributions.

256.200 Neglecting collective efforts sows the seeds of division and resentment.

512.399 Ensure that all contributions are recognized and cherished.

512.400 Address issues of exclusion and promote inclusivity.

## 64.51 Strive for Perfection

### 128.101 CONTINUOUS IMPROVEMENT:

256.201 The pursuit of continuous improvement is the path to excellence and growth.

512.401 Encourage a mindset of lifelong learning and self-betterment.

512.402 Provide resources for both personal and professional development.

256.202 Complacency is the mire that leads to stagnation and mediocrity.

512.403 Confront complacency with motivation and the spark of ambition.

512.404 Reward efforts that embody the spirit of continuous improvement.

### 128.102 PURSUE EXCELLENCE:

256.203 The quest for excellence in all endeavors enriches life and achievement.

512.405 Cultivate a culture of high standards and exceptional quality.

512.406 Celebrate and honor excellence within the citizenry.

256.204 Settling for mediocrity diminishes potential and fulfillment.

512.407 Illuminate the importance of striving for one's best.

512.408 Support the journey toward personal and communal excellence.

## 64.52 Align with the Will of All

### 128.103 SEEK COLLECTIVE GOOD:

256.205 Encourage practices that prioritize the citizenry's well-being.

512.409 Champion the individual as the bedrock of society.

512.410 Recognize and reward contributions to the collective good.

256.206 Irrational actions lead to division and conflict.

512.411 Address and educate on the impacts of irrational behaviors.

512.412 Promote a culture of rational self-interest that benefits the whole.

### 128.104 UNDERSTAND UNIVERSAL WILL:

256.207 Striving to understand and align with the collective will fosters unity.

512.413 Offer discussions and trainings on understanding the collective will.

512.414 Encourage reflection on how individual actions impact the citizenry.

256.208 Ignoring the universal will leads to disconnection and discord.

512.415 Address issues of misalignment with the collective will.

512.416 Provide support for aligning personal actions with communal goals.

## 64.53 Respect Nature

### 128.105 LIVE HARMONIOUSLY WITH NATURE:

256.209 Living harmoniously with nature ensures sustainability and balance.

512.417 Promote practices that protect and sustain the natural environment.

512.418 Educate on the importance of ecological balance and conservation.

256.210 Disrespect for nature leads to environmental degradation and imbalance.

512.419 Address and correct behaviors that harm the environment.

512.420 Provide resources for sustainable living and environmental stewardship.

### 128.106 PROTECT THE ENVIRONMENT:

256.211 Actively engaging in environmental protection preserves natural resources.

512.421 Create initiatives for citizenry participation in environmental protection.

512.422 Recognize and reward efforts toward environmental conservation.

256.212 Neglecting the environment results in loss of biodiversity and ecological crisis.

512.423 Educate on the impacts of environmental neglect and promote action.

512.424 Provide support for citizenry-driven environmental projects.

## 64.54 Value Hard Work

### 128.107 COMMIT TO EFFORT:

256.213 Recognizing the importance of hard work leads to success and fulfillment.

512.425 Encourage a strong work ethic and dedication to tasks.

512.426 Provide opportunities for skill development and hard work.

256.214 Avoiding effort results in mediocrity and unrealized potential.

512.427 Address issues of laziness and lack of motivation with support.

512.428 Promote activities that require and teach the value of hard work.

### 128.108 REWARD DILIGENCE:

256.215 Appreciating and rewarding hard work fosters motivation and achievement.

512.429 Recognize and celebrate the efforts and achievements of hard-working individuals.

512.430 Create systems for fair and meaningful rewards for diligence.

256.216 Ignoring diligence leads to discouragement and lack of productivity.

512.431 Ensure that diligent efforts are consistently acknowledged.

512.432 Address issues of lack of recognition and promote a culture of appreciation.

## 64.55 Encourage Civic Responsibility

### 128.109 PARTICIPATE ACTIVELY:

256.217 Engaging in citizenry activities strengthens civic responsibility.

512.433 Promote volunteerism and active participation in citizenry events.

512.434 Provide opportunities for civic engagement and leadership.

256.218 Apathy toward citizenry involvement weakens societal bonds.

512.435 Address issues of apathy with motivation and education.

512.436 Recognize and reward active participation and civic contributions.

### 128.110 PROMOTE CITIZENRY WELFARE:

256.219 Advocating for citizenry welfare ensures a supportive and thriving society.

512.437 Encourage policies and practices that prioritize citizenry well-being.

512.438 Support initiatives that address social issues and promote welfare.

256.220 Neglecting citizenry welfare leads to social issues and disintegration.

512.439 Educate on the importance of citizenry welfare and involvement.

512.440 Provide resources for improving and supporting citizenry welfare.

## 64.56 Value Merit

### 128.111 RECOGNIZE ACHIEVEMENT:

256.221 To exalt merit and achievement is to sow the seeds of excellence and fairness.

512.441 Establish realms where the laurels of merit are bestowed and celebrated.

512.442 Foster a culture that cherishes toil and honors accomplishments.

256.222 The neglect of merit begets favoritism and saps the spirit.

512.443 Confront and correct favoritism, ensuring that merit shines brightly.

512.444 Teach the sacredness of recognizing true merit.

### 128.112 PROMOTE MERITOCRACY:

256.223 A system rooted in merit ensures a harvest of equal opportunities and just rewards.

512.445 Enact laws that uphold and promote the doctrine of meritocracy.

512.446 Encourage practices that guarantee fair and equal chances for all souls.

256.224 The rejection of meritocracy breeds inequality and discord.

512.447 Dismantle barriers to merit with the tools of education and support.

512.448 Cultivate a culture that esteems fairness and equal pathways to triumph.

## 64.57 Promote Critical Thinking

### 128.113 USE REASON:

256.225 To champion reason and logic is to pave the way for wise decisions.

512.449 Offer teachings in the arts of logic, critical thought, and the crafting of wise choices.

512.450 Nurture spaces for rational discourse and analytic problem-solving.

256.226 The abandonment of reason leads to folly and error.

512.451 Correct the missteps of poor judgment with the lantern of education.

512.452 Provide resources to sharpen and refine the skills of reasoning.

### 128.114 QUESTION ASSUMPTIONS:

256.227 The practice of questioning assumptions births deeper understanding.

512.453 Encourage a spirit of inquiry and the critical appraisal of accepted truths.

512.454 Create avenues for introspection and reassessment.

256.228 Accepting assumptions without scrutiny leads to bias and error.

512.455 Illuminate the perils of unchallenged assumptions and ingrained biases.

512.456 Foster a culture of relentless inquiry and perpetual learning.

## 64.58 Uphold Individual Rights

### 128.115 DEFEND FREEDOMS:

256.229 To champion the sanctity of personal liberties is to ensure the freedom of both the individual and society.

512.457 Illuminate the populace on the vital essence of personal rights and the liberties that guard our civilization.

512.458 Assemble bands of advocates to shield and uphold the cause of personal freedoms.

256.230 The neglect of individual rights beckons the shadow of oppression and the blight of injustice.

512.459 Swiftly and justly confront breaches against these sacred rights.

512.460 Endorse policies that enshrine and protect personal liberties.

### 128.116 PROMOTE JUSTICE:

256.231 Upholding the rights of each soul fosters a realm of equity and righteousness.

512.461 Establish systems of law and society that stand as pillars of justice.

512.462 Honor and commend those who advance and safeguard the cause of justice.

256.232 The abandonment of justice gives rise to disparity and strife.

512.463 Teach the dire consequences of injustice and foster a culture of accountability.

512.464 Support endeavors that fortify the foundations of justice.

## 64.59 Respect Property

### 128.117 HONOR OWNERSHIP:

256.233 To honor the rights of ownership is to cultivate trust and a sense of duty.

512.465 Enlighten on the significance of property rights and the stewardship they demand.

512.466 Devise equitable systems to resolve disputes over ownership.

256.234 The disrespect of property rights sows the seeds of discord and legal turmoil.

512.467 Address and rectify infringements upon property rights with justice.

512.468 Nurture a culture that respects ownership and the responsibilities it entails.

### 128.118 ENCOURAGE RESPONSIBILITY:

256.235 The mindful use of property ensures its preservation and care.

512.469 Advocate for sustainable practices and responsible stewardship.

512.470 Acknowledge and reward those who manage property with wisdom and care.

256.236 The neglectful use of property leads to its desolation and waste.

512.471 Confront issues of neglect and waste through education and support.

512.472 Champion initiatives that inspire care and sustainable use.

## 64.60 Support Scientific Inquiry

### 128.119 ENCOURAGE EXPLORATION:

256.237 Embrace the quest for knowledge, for it brings forth discovery and the light of progress.

512.473 Establish sanctuaries for the pursuit of wisdom and the birth of innovation.

512.474 Illuminate minds on the virtues of inquiry and the pursuit of truth through evidence and reason.

256.238 To stifle exploration is to dim the beacon of advancement and ingenuity.

512.475 Tear down the walls that hinder the journey of the mind, offering aid and guidance.

512.476 Cultivate a realm where curiosity is the seed and discovery the fruit.

### 128.120 PROMOTE INNOVATION:

256.239 A garden that nurtures the seeds of inquiry shall bloom with the flowers of technological and intellectual prowess.

512.477 Foster a symphony between the minds of scientists and the hearts of the citizenry.

512.478 Exalt the achievements of those who chart the unknown and contribute to the eternal scroll of knowledge.

256.240 Forsaking the march of progress leads to the mire of stagnation and the abyss of regression.

512.479 Bestow upon the seekers the tools to remain vigilant in the ever-flowing river of advancement.

512.480 Confront the shadows of neglect with the light of education and unwavering support.

## 64.61 Deal with Enemies of the Way

### 128.121 IDENTIFY AND CONFRONT ENEMIES:

256.241 Acknowledge that the foes of the Way are the servants of None, worthy of no mercy.

512.481 Forge strategies with the fires of resolve to unmask and confront these adversaries.

512.482 Stand ever watchful, guarding the sanctity of the Way against all threats.

256.242 Confront the harbingers of darkness with an unyielding spirit.

512.483 Train in the arts of strategy and strength to vanquish the foes that arise.

512.484 Embody actions that reflect the power and steadfastness of our cause.

### 128.122 JUSTIFIED DESTRUCTION:

256.243 The enemies of the Way, heralds of chaos, must be eradicated to preserve order.

512.485 Sanction actions that obliterate these threats, ensuring the dominion of the Way remains unchallenged.

512.486 Foster a culture of vigilance and readiness, ever prepared for the battle against the void.

256.244 The annihilation of malevolence is necessary to uphold the harmony of existence.

512.487 Master the methods of decisive confrontation.

512.488 Encourage deeds that support the purging of threats, maintaining the purity of our sacred order.

## 64.62 Be Organized

### 128.123 EMBRACE STRUCTURED LIVING:

256.245 Recognize the power of organization in achieving the goals of the Way.

512.489 Develop systems that streamline daily activities, enhancing efficiency and productivity.

512.490 Maintain order in all aspects of life, from personal spaces to communal environments.

256.246 Cultivate habits that promote discipline and structure.

512.491 Implement routines that reinforce consistency and stability.

512.492 Encourage practices that foster clarity and focus in all endeavors.

### 128.124 FOSTER STRATEGIC PLANNING:

256.247 Acknowledge the importance of foresight and preparation in the path of the Way.

512.493 Create comprehensive plans that anticipate challenges and outline clear steps to overcome them.

512.494 Utilize tools and technologies that aid in effective planning and execution.

256.248 Develop a mindset oriented toward continuous improvement and optimization.

512.495 Regularly review and adjust strategies to ensure alignment with long-term objectives.

512.496 Encourage feedback and collaboration to refine and enhance organizational practices.

## 64.63 Communicate Effectively

### 128.125 EMBRACE EFFECTIVE COMMUNICATION:

256.249 Recognize the significance of effective communication in fostering understanding.

512.497 Build strong relationships through genuine affinity and empathy.

512.498 Establish a shared reality by finding common ground and mutual understanding.

256.250 Master the art of effective communication.

512.499 Develop clear and concise communication skills to convey ideas and intentions accurately.

512.500 Listen actively and respond thoughtfully to foster meaningful interactions.

### 128.126 ENHANCE INTERPERSONAL CONNECTIONS:

256.251 Utilize the principles of effective communication to strengthen bonds within the citizenry.

512.501 Encourage open and honest dialogue to resolve conflicts and build trust.

512.502 Promote a culture of collaboration and support through effective communication.

256.252 Foster an environment where communication flourishes.

512.503 Implement systems and practices that facilitate seamless information sharing and understanding.

512.504 Encourage ongoing learning and development to enhance communication skills within the citizenry.

## 64.64 Our Destiny Is the Cosmos

### 128.127 EMBRACE THE FRONTIER OF SPACE:

256.253 Mankind's destiny lies in the stars.

512.505 Promote the reality that man is destined to conquer the cosmos.

512.506 Foster a pioneering spirit that embraces challenges and seeks new opportunities.

256.254 Prepare for the physical and psychological demands of space colonization.

512.507 Train individuals in the necessary skills and knowledge for successful colonization.

512.508 Promote resilience and adaptability to thrive in the unknown realms of space.

### 128.128 ESTABLISH NEW COMMUNITIES:

256.255 Create self-sufficient colonies that reflect the principles of the Way.

512.509 Design infrastructure and systems that support sustainable living and growth.

512.510 Maintain the Scribe's order throughout the cosmos.

256.256 Foster a culture of exploration and discovery.

512.511 Encourage scientific research and innovation to overcome the challenges of space colonization.

512.512 Promote the continuous pursuit of knowledge and advancement for the betterment of all.

1024

# OTHER BOOKS PUBLISHED BY ARKTOS

| | |
|---|---|
| Virginia Abernethy | Born Abroad |
| Sri Dharma Pravartaka Acharya | The Dharma Manifesto |
| Joakim Andersen | Rising from the Ruins |
| Winston C. Banks | Excessive Immigration |
| Stephen Baskerville | Who Lost America? |
| Alfred Baeumler | Nietzsche: Philosopher and Politician |
| Alain de Benoist | Beyond Human Rights |
| | Carl Schmitt Today |
| | The Ideology of Sameness |
| | The Indo-Europeans |
| | Manifesto for a European Renaissance |
| | On the Brink of the Abyss |
| | The Problem of Democracy |
| | Runes and the Origins of Writing |
| | View from the Right (vol. 1–3) |
| Armand Berger | Tolkien, Europe, and Tradition |
| Arthur Moeller van den Bruck | Germany's Third Empire |
| Matt Battaglioli | The Consequences of Equality |
| Kerry Bolton | The Perversion of Normality |
| | Revolution from Above |
| | Yockey: A Fascist Odyssey |
| Isac Boman | Money Power |
| Charles William Dailey | The Serpent Symbol in Tradition |
| Ricardo Duchesne | Faustian Man in a Multicultural Age |
| Alexander Dugin | Ethnos and Society |
| | Ethnosociology |
| | Eurasian Mission |
| | The Fourth Political Theory |
| | The Great Awakening vs the Great Reset |
| | Last War of the World-Island |
| | Politica Aeterna |
| | Political Platonism |
| | Putin vs Putin |
| | The Rise of the Fourth Political Theory |
| | Templars of the Proletariat |
| | The Theory of a Multipolar World |
| Daria Dugina | A Theory of Europe |
| Edward Dutton | Race Differences in Ethnocentrism |
| Mark Dyal | Hated and Proud |
| Clare Ellis | The Blackening of Europe |
| Koenraad Elst | Return of the Swastika |
| Julius Evola | The Bow and the Club |
| | Fascism Viewed from the Right |
| | A Handbook for Right-Wing Youth |
| | Metaphysics of Power |
| | Metaphysics of War |
| | The Myth of the Blood |
| | Notes on the Third Reich |

# OTHER BOOKS PUBLISHED BY ARKTOS

|  |  |
|---|---|
|  | *Pagan Imperialism* |
|  | *Recognitions* |
|  | *A Traditionalist Confronts Fascism* |
| GUILLAUME FAYE | *Archeofuturism* |
|  | *Archeofuturism 2.0* |
|  | *The Colonisation of Europe* |
|  | *Convergence of Catastrophes* |
|  | *Ethnic Apocalypse* |
|  | *A Global Coup* |
|  | *Prelude to War* |
|  | *Sex and Deviance* |
|  | *Understanding Islam* |
|  | *Why We Fight* |
| DANIEL S. FORREST | *Suprahumanism* |
| ANDREW FRASER | *Dissident Dispatches* |
|  | *Reinventing Aristocracy in the Age of Woke Capital* |
|  | *The WASP Question* |
| GÉNÉRATION IDENTITAIRE | *We are Generation Identity* |
| PETER GOODCHILD | *The Taxi Driver from Baghdad* |
|  | *The Western Path* |
| PAUL GOTTFRIED | *War and Democracy* |
| PETR HAMPL | *Breached Enclosure* |
| PORUS HOMI HAVEWALA | *The Saga of the Aryan Race* |
| LARS HOLGER HOLM | *Hiding in Broad Daylight* |
|  | *Homo Maximus* |
|  | *Incidents of Travel in Latin America* |
|  | *The Owls of Afrasiab* |
| RICHARD HOUCK | *Liberalism Unmasked* |
| A. J. ILLINGWORTH | *Political Justice* |
| INSTITUT ILIADE | *For a European Awakening* |
|  | *Guardians of Heritage* |
| ALEXANDER JACOB | *De Naturae Natura* |
| JASON REZA JORJANI | *Artemis Unveiled* |
|  | *Closer Encounters* |
|  | *Erosophia* |
|  | *Faustian Futurist* |
|  | *Iranian Leviathan* |
|  | *Lovers of Sophia* |
|  | *Novel Folklore* |
|  | *Philosophy of the Future* |
|  | *Prometheism* |
|  | *Promethean Pirate* |
|  | *Prometheus and Atlas* |
|  | *Psychotron* |
|  | *Uber Man* |
|  | *World State of Emergency* |
| HENRIK JONASSON | *Sigmund* |
| EDGAR JULIUS JUNG | *The Significance of the German Revolution* |

# OTHER BOOKS PUBLISHED BY ARKTOS

| | |
|---|---|
| Ruuben Kaalep & August Meister | Rebirth of Europe |
| Roderick Kaine | Smart and SeXy |
| Peter King | Here and Now |
| | Keeping Things Close |
| | On Modern Manners |
| James Kirkpatrick | Conservatism Inc. |
| Ludwig Klages | The Biocentric Worldview |
| | Cosmogonic Reflections |
| | The Science of Character |
| Andrew Korybko | Hybrid Wars |
| Pierre Krebs | Guillaume Faye: Truths & Tributes |
| | Fighting for the Essence |
| Julien Langella | Catholic and Identitarian |
| John Bruce Leonard | The New Prometheans |
| Diana Panchenko | The Inevitable |
| Stephen Pax Leonard | The Ideology of Failure |
| | Travels in Cultural Nihilism |
| William S. Lind | Reforging Excalibur |
| | Retroculture |
| Pentti Linkola | Can Life Prevail? |
| Giorgio Locchi | Definitions |
| H. P. Lovecraft | The Conservative |
| Norman Lowell | Imperium Europa |
| Richard Lynn | Sex Differences in Intelligence |
| | A Tribute to Helmut Nyborg (ed.) |
| John MacLugash | The Return of the Solar King |
| Charles Maurras | The Future of the Intelligentsia & |
| | For a French Awakening |
| John Harmon McElroy | Agitprop in America |
| Michael O'Meara | Guillaume Faye and the Battle of Europe |
| | New Culture, New Right |
| Michael Millerman | Beginning with Heidegger |
| Dmitry Moiseev | The Philosophy of Italian Fascism |
| Maurice Muret | The Greatness of Elites |
| Brian Anse Patrick | The NRA and the Media |
| | Rise of the Anti-Media |
| | The Ten Commandments of Propaganda |
| | Zombology |
| Tito Perdue | The Bent Pyramid |
| | Journey to a Location |
| | Lee |
| | Morning Crafts |
| | Philip |
| | The Sweet-Scented Manuscript |
| | William's House (vol. 1–4) |
| John K. Press | The True West vs the Zombie Apocalypse |
| Raido | A Handbook of Traditional Living (vol. 1–2) |

# OTHER BOOKS PUBLISHED BY ARKTOS

| | |
|---|---|
| P R Reddall | *Towards Awakening* |
| Claire Rae Randall | *The War on Gender* |
| Steven J. Rosen | *The Agni and the Ecstasy* |
| | *The Jedi in the Lotus* |
| Nicholas Rooney | *Talking to the Wolf* |
| Richard Rudgley | *Barbarians* |
| | *Essential Substances* |
| | *Wildest Dreams* |
| Ernst von Salomon | *It Cannot Be Stormed* |
| | *The Outlaws* |
| Werner Sombart | *Traders and Heroes* |
| Piero San Giorgio | *Giuseppe* |
| | *Survive the Economic Collapse* |
| | *Surviving the Next Catastrophe* |
| Sri Sri Ravi Shankar | *Celebrating Silence* |
| | *Know Your Child* |
| | *Management Mantras* |
| | *Patanjali Yoga Sutras* |
| | *Secrets of Relationships* |
| George T. Shaw (ed.) | *A Fair Hearing* |
| Fenek Solère | *Kraal* |
| | *Reconquista* |
| Oswald Spengler | *The Decline of the West* |
| | *Man and Technics* |
| Richard Storey | *The Uniqueness of Western Law* |
| Tomislav Sunic | *Against Democracy and Equality* |
| | *Homo Americanus* |
| | *Postmortem Report* |
| | *Titans are in Town* |
| Askr Svarte | *Gods in the Abyss* |
| Hans-Jürgen Syberberg | *On the Fortunes and Misfortunes of Art in Post-War Germany* |
| Abir Taha | *Defining Terrorism* |
| | *The Epic of Arya* (2nd ed.) |
| | *Nietzsche is Coming God, or the Redemption of the Divine* |
| | *Verses of Light* |
| Jean Thiriart | *Europe: An Empire of 400 Million* |
| Bal Gangadhar Tilak | *The Arctic Home in the Vedas* |
| Dominique Venner | *Ernst Jünger: A Different European Destiny* |
| | *For a Positive Critique* |
| | *The Shock of History* |
| Hans Vogel | *How Europe Became American* |
| Markus Willinger | *A Europe of Nations* |
| | *Generation Identity* |
| Alexander Wolfheze | *Alba Rosa* |
| | *Globus Horribilis* |
| | *Rupes Nigra* |

www.ingramcontent.com/pod-product-compliance
Lightning Source LLC
Chambersburg PA
CBHW031433160426
43195CB00010BB/719